Over 225 years of Keys/ Keyes

Over 225 years of Keys/ Keyes Families in Eastern North Carolina

By Bunyon Keys

A Native son of Blounts Creek

Bunyon Keys

Copyright © 2018 by Bunyon Keys.

Library of Congress Control Number: 2018905067
ISBN: Hardcover   978-1-9845-2438-6
                Softcover   978-1-9845-2439-3
                eBook   978-1-9845-2437-9

All rights reserved. No part of this book may be reproduced or transmitted in any form or by any means, electronic or mechanical, including photocopying, recording, or by any information storage and retrieval system, without permission in writing from the copyright owner.

Any people depicted in stock imagery provided by Getty Images are models, and such images are being used for illustrative purposes only.
Certain stock imagery © Getty Images.

Print information available on the last page.

Rev. date: 05/31/2018

To order additional copies of this book, contact:
Xlibris
1-888-795-4274
www.Xlibris.com
Orders@Xlibris.com
541424

Contents

Foreword xv

Chapter 1

Section I Part A Overview 1
Section II Part A Milley's Children 2
Section II Part B Amy Keys and Willoughby Moore 4
Section II Part C Nancy Keys 4
Section II Part C-2 Southey Keys 4
Section II Part C-3 Sara Keys and March Stilley 5
Section II Part C-3-2 Zachariah (Zach) Stilley and Lydia Ann Moore 6
Section II Part C-3-3 Lewis Johnson Stilley and Henrietta Pike 6
Section II Part C-3-4 Olivia Stilley and Stephen Little 6
Section II Part C-3-5 Frank Stilley 7
Section II Part C-3-6 Mary Stilley and James Gardner 7
Section II Part D Charity (Clary) Keys 8
Section II Part E Lucy Keys 8
Section II Part E-2 John Keys and Emerline Grice 9
Section II Part E-2-2 William Keys and Evalina E Hunter 9
Section II Part E-2-2-2 Della Keys and Joseph Payton 9
Section II Part F Silvy (Sebry) Keys 10
Section II Part F-2 Zack Keys and Mary Keys 10
Section II Part G Wyatt Keys (Keas) and Jeliky Rhodes 11
Section II Part H Malachi Keys 11
Section II Part H-2 Malachi (Maliki) Keys and Penny Keys/Nelly Keys 11

Chapter 2

Section I Part A Sally Keys 13
Section II Part A John Keys and Mary Keys 13
Section II Part B John Jr. Keys and Nancy Keys 13
Section III Part A 1st Bannon Keyes and Peggy a Moore 13
Section III Part B Lacy Keyes and Estelle Williams 14
Section III Part B-2 Gus Keyes and Hansel L Moore 14

Section III Part B-3 Peggy Keyes and John Harold Peterson 15
Section III Part B-4 John Earl Keyes and Lizena O'Neal 15
Section III Part B-5 Mattie R Keyes and Linwood Martin 15
Section III Part B-6 Doris Keyes and Thomas Jr. Myer 16
Section III Part C Tinsey Keyes and Leroy Moore 17
Section III Part D Southey (Susie) (Suzzy) Keyes and Betty/
    Lillian/Jasper Smith 17
Section III Part E Simon (Booth) Keyes and Maggie Moore 18
Section IV Part A Isaiah Keys and Freddia A Moore/Peggy Moore 18
Section IV Part B Fevby (Ferraby) Keys and Alonzo Blango 19

Chapter 3

Section I Part A William Keys and Mary Thornton 20
Section II Part A Lydia Keys and Giles (Gent Giles) Moore 21
Section II Part B Descendants of Peggy Moore and James H
    Moore/Isaiah Keys 21
Section II Part C Mary Moore and Israel Moore 22
Section II Part D William Plas and Sara Ann Lindsey 22
Section II Part D-2 Henry Moore and Della Aldridge 22
Section II Part D-2-2 Roosevelt Moore and Melvina Moore 23
Section II Part D-2-3 Noah E Moore and Jennie Moore 24
Section II Part D-2-4 Worstey (Vaster) Moore and Major Birt 24
Section II Part D-2-5 Purl (Pearlier) Moore and John Keys 24
Section II Part D-2-6 Tiny Moore and Bessie Moore/Neta Moore ... 25
Section II Part D-2-7 Joshua B Moore and Georgianna Kinsey 26
Section III Part A Grace Keys and Giles (Gent Giles) Moore 26
Section III Part B Descendants of James E. Keys and Harriett Johnson....26
Section III Part B-2 James E Keyes II and Eva Mitchell 27
Section III Part B-2-2 Garfield Keyes and Emma Moore/Mary
    Stilley Crawford 27
Section III Part B-2-3 Hattie Keyes and James H Foskey 28
Section III Part B-2-4 Gertrude Keyes and Thelmon Moore 28
Section III Part B-2-5 James E. Keyes III and Hilda Gaye 29
Section III Part B-3 Elizabeth Keys and Phillip Keys 29
Section III Part B-3-2 Kessiah Keys and Joe Johnson 29

Section III Part B-4 Orlando Keys and Carrie Stilley 30
Section III Part B-4-2 Booker T. Keys and Grace Moore 30
Section III Part B-4-3 Lula M. Keys and Golden C Hudgins 31
Section III Part B-4-4 Jessie M Keys and John H Smith 31
Section III Part B-4-5 Earl Lee Keys and Benjamin (Ben) Oden 31
Section III Part B-5 Grace Keys and James Allen Moore 32
Section III Part C Mary Jane Keys (went by her middle name
    Jean) and James Milton Moore 32
Section III Part C-2 William Moore and Roxanna Mitchell 33
Section III Part C-2-3 Civy I Moore and Abner Keys 33
Section III Part C-2-4 Annie Keys and Sylvester Washington 34
Section III Part C-2-5 Margie Keys and John Smith............................. 34
Section III Part C-3 Elijah Moore and Lina Moore 34
Section III Part C-4 Israel Moore and 2nd Laura Wilson 35
Section III Part C-4-2 3rd Laura Moore and Nathan Hooker 36
Section III Part C-4-3 James H Moore and Clara Moore...................... 36
Section III Part C-4-4 Climmie Moore and Dewitt Moore 36
Section III Part C-4-5 Minnie C Moore and William David Moore 37
Section III Part D Bannon Moore and Margaret Blango 37
Section IIII Part D-2 Betsey A Moore and Jesse Moore 38
Section III Part D-2-2 Mahue Moore and Edna Roberson 38
Section III Part D-2-3 Willie Moore and Maud Holiday/
    Mulgray Johnson 38
Section III D-2-4 William E Moore and Ledell Smith............................ 39
Section III Part D-2-5 Ella M Moore and Norman Walter Welch 39
Section III Part D-3 James E Moore and Cora L Williams..................... 40
Section III Part D-3-2 Bannon Moore and Idessa Moore...................... 40
Section III Part D-3-3 McQuinton Moore and Lucy Moore 41
Section III Part D-3-4 Eugene Moore 41
Section III Part D-3-5 Anna L Moor... 41
Section III Part D-3-6 James M Moore and Rebecca Ham 42
Section III Part D-3-7 Archie D (Kelly) Moore andCoreen Smith 42
Section III Part E Elizabeth (Lizzie) Moore and Josephus Keys 42
Section III Part F Clara Moore and James E Moore.............................. 43
Section III Part G Dewitt Moore and Climmie Moore 43

Section III Part H Sara (Little Sara) Moore and Emanuel Moore 43
Section II Part I David Moore and Lottie Smith 43
Section III Part J William Arthur Moore and Cora J. Peacock 44
Section III Part K Milton (Jr) Moore and Georgiana Moore 44
Section III Part L Emanuel Moore and Melissa Keys 44
Section III Part L-2 Lincey Moore and Bethany Blango 45
Section III Part L-3 Roscoe Moore and Elizabeth Moore 45
Section III Part M Lincey C Moore and Cora Williams Moore 46
Section III Part M-2 Cora O Moore and William W Little 46
Section III Part N Sara (Big Sara) Moore and Filbert Swindell/
    Thomas (Shake) Little 46
Section III Part N-2 Theodore Swindell and Lillian Hudgins 47
Section III Part N-3 Gaynell Swindell and Percy Edward Brown 47
Section III Part O Emanuel (Little Emanuel) Moore and Sara Moore ... 48
Section III Part P Vinettie Moore and David Minor 48
Section IV Part A William (Jr.) Keys and Visa Keys 48
Section IV Part B Charles Keys Sr. and Tamar Bell/Martha Blunt 49
Section IV Part B-2 Carrie Carolina Keys and John A Dixon 50
Section IV Part B-3 Ella/Ellen Keys and David Coward 50
Section IV Part B-4 Amandia (Amanda) Keys and Henry J Keys 50
Section IV Part B-5 Charles Keys Jr. and Daisy Dudley/Charity
    King/Chole Lane 51
Section IV Part B-6 Florence Keyes and J D Aldridge 51
Section IV Part B-7 Mary J Keyes 52
Section IV Part B-8 Anita (Netey) Keyes and George A Lindsey 52
Section IV Part B-9 Lola Keyes and J D Wallace 52
Section IV Part B-9-2 Delzora Wallace and Hullis Jenkins 53
Section IV Part B-9-3 Bessie Wallace and Amos Dawson 53
Section IV Part B-9-4 Charley R Wallace and Ollie L Harris 53
Section IV Part B-9-4 Dempsey Wallace and Clemmie Ethel Nobles ... 54
Section IV Part B-10 Sadie Keyes and Joseph A Latham 54
Section IV Part B-10-2 Vera M Latham and Harvey Tyree 54
Section IV Part B-10-3 Joseph C Latham and Hattie Lucille Moore 55
Section IV Part B-11 Bertha Keyes and William A Yates 55
Section IV Part B-11-2 Matthew H Yates and Mabel Latham 55

Section IV Part B-12 Bessie Keyes and Israel Moore 56
Section IV Part B-12-2 Annie L Moore and Ernest Simmons 56
Section IV Part B-12-3 Charles L Moore and Geraldine Moore 56
Section IV Part B-12-4 Elizabeth Moore and Robert Jordan 57
Section IV Part B-12-5 George A Moore and Elizabeth Smith 57
Section IV Part B-12-5-2 Florine Moore and Jeffery Bragg 57
Section IV Part B-13 Mattie L Keyes and William Joseph Moore 58
Section V Part A Caroline Keys and James H Yates 58
Section V Part A-2 John H Yates and Emma Dixon 58
Section V Part A-3 Sally A Yates and Henry Bell 59
Section V Part A Laura Keys and Henry Jones 59

Chapter 4

Section I Part A Milley Keys 60
Section II Part A Isaiah (Isiac) Keys and Rebecca Wiggins................... 60
Section II Part B William Keys and Clarisa Chatman/Mamie Keys 60
Section II Part B-2 Gertrude Keys and Willie Weeks........................... 61
Section II Part B-3 Richard Keys and Mabelle Ackiss 61
Section II Part B-4 Oliver Keys and Ada Clark 61
Section III Part A Milley Keys 62
Section III Part B Miles Keys and Nancy Wilkins.................................. 62
Section III Part C Annice (Annie) (Walker) Keys and Nathan Keys 62
Section III Part C-2 Allace Keys and Allen Payton................................ 63
Section III Part C-3 William H Keys and Sadie (Suddia) Bembry........... 63
Section IV Part A Mary Keys and Augusta Wilkins 63

Chapter 5

Section I Part A Mary Keys 64
Section II Part B Lacy Keys and Mary Keys 64
Section II Part B-2 Daniel Keys and Mary E Moore.............................. 64
Section II Part B-2-3 Daniel S Keys and Lillian Keys............................. 65
Section II Part C Simon Keys and Cornelia Morgan 65
Section III Part A John Keys and Frances Keys 65
Section III Part B Southey Keyes (Keese) 66

Section III Part C Zachariah Keyes 66
Section III Part C-2 2nd Bannon (Banner) Keyes and Peggy Moore 66
Section III Part C-2-2 William C (Kam) Keyes and Carrie
           Foreman/Doris Cratch/Willie J Cobb................................. 67
Section III Part C-2-2-2 Mattie Keyes and Linwood Martin 68
Section III Part C-2-2-5 William Isiah Keyes and Ethel L Godley 68
Section III Part C-2-2-8 Francis (Layhu) Keyes and Alonza
           Elijah Moore/SG Gardner 68
Section III Part C-2-2-10 Edward Keyes and Vienna Moore 69
Section III Part D John Keyes and Annie Latham/Emma Tuten 69
Section III Part E David Keyes and Eliza B Keyes 70
Section IV Part A James Keys and Nancy Moore..................................... 70
Section IV Part B William Keys and Tamar Stilley 71
Section IV Part B-2 Minnie Keys and William A Moore 71
Section IV Part B-3 Thurston Keys and Minnie Moore 71
Section IV Part B-4 Malachi Keys and Jessie F Moore 72
Section IV Part B-4-2 Almeta Keys and David Moore.............................. 72
Section IV Part B-4-3 Hazel Keys and James A Moore 72
Section IV Part B-4-4 Rumley Keys and Bedie B 73
Section IV Part B-4-4-2 James A Keys and Roberta Stilley 73
Section IV Part C James Keys JR. and Nancy A Moore 73
Section IV Part D Benjamin (Ben) keys and Rhoda Pierce 74
Section IV Part E Mary Keys and William B Brown 74
Section IV Part F Annie Keys and Ephraim William Copeland............... 74
Section IV Part G Simon Keys and Laura Grist/Sara J Wilkins 75
Section IV Part I Ivry (Ivory) Keys and Margaret Boyed 75
Section IV Part K-3 Frank Copeland and Helen Marie Pierce 75
Section V Part A (Mamie) Mary S Moore and James H Moore.............. 76
Section V Part B Bertha A Moore and Israel Smith 76
Section V Part C Mary L Moore and Ralph Boskey/Willie Joyner 76

Chapter 6

Section I Part A Mary Keys 78
Section II Part B Lewis Keyes and Sallie (Sara) A Moore 78
Section II Part C Nancy Keyes and John Taper/Frank Brooks............... 79

Section II Part C-2 John T Taper and Katie H James 80
Section II Part C-2-2 Lena Taper and Solomon Hodge 80
Section II Part C-2-3 Johnnie Taper and Indiana Boston 80
Section II Part C-2-4 Ada Taper and Collins/James E Tyner/
    Warren W Brooks 81
Section II Part C-2-5 Clarence Taper and Mittie Boston 81
Section II Part C-2-6 Gladys Taper and Abraham Pierce 82
Section II Part D Christopher C Keyes and Sophia Peele/
    Florence Gaylord 82
Section II Part D-2 Christopher F Keyes and Elizabeth Pawell 83
Section II Part D-2-2 Mary Marie Keyes and Jasper (Joseph) Smith 84
Section II Part D-2-3 Christen Keyes and Matthew Lewis 84
Section II Part E Charles H Keyes and Alberta Griffin 85
Section II Part F Sara (Sadie) Keyes and Job Daniel/Henry Moore 85
Section II Part F-2 Mary Alvania Moore and Thadious K
    (T.K.) Woolard 86
Section II Part G Mamie Keyes and Mack D Woolard 86
Section II Part H Rudella Keyes and William Bruce Boston 86
Section II Part I Lena C Keyes and Andrew Jones 87
Section II Part J Rosa F Keyes and George Hardison 87
Section III Part A Sara Elizabeth Keyes and Benjamin Boston 88
Section III Part B Wills Boston and Essie Boston (Esell Barton) 88
Section III Part B-2 Dollie E Boston and Willie Brooks 89
Section III Part B-3 Benjamin F Boston and Hattie Wallace 89
Section III Part B-4 Manford Boston and Edith Pitman 89
Section III Part B-5 Irene Boston and Nathaniel Bonds 90
Section III Part B-6 Noah Boston and Virginia Sykes.......................... 90
Section III Part B-7 James E Boston and Mercy D Moore 90
Section III Part B-8 Ophelia Boston and Elmond A James 91
Section III Part B-9 Sylvania Boston and Homer H Gee 91
Section IV Part A Ivory V Keyes and Margaret E Boston/
    Nancy D Barber 91
Section IV Part B Benjamin Franklin Keyes and Beatrice
    (Bertie) F Smith 92
Section IV Part C Walter Raleigh Keyes and Minna G Hill 92

Section IV Part D Dora J Keyes and Wilford Staton 93
Section IV Part E William S Keyes and Estella James 93
Section IV Part F James H. Keyes and Hazel M Credle........................ 93
Section IV Part G Ivory J Keyes and Viola Ward 94
Section IV Part H Lewellyn Keyes and Addie L James 94
Section V Part A Robert Keyes and Harriet Moore............................... 94
Section V Part A-2 Sadie (Sallie) Keyes and James Ruffin 95
Section V Part B J F (Frank) Keyes and Mattie Ebron 95
Section VI Part C Kizziah (Kezzia) Keyes 96
Section VI Part C-2 Lewis Keyes and Sallie Pierce 96
Section VI Part C-3 Hattie Keyes and Rufus Hodge 96
Section VI Part C-4 Mollie Keyes and James Matthew Pierce 97
Section VII Part A Charles Keyes and Diane Riggs............................... 97
Section VIII Part A Frank J Keyes and Claudia Lilley 97

Chapter 7

Section I Part A Joseph Keyes and Kezzia Little 99
Section II Part A Mary Keyes Moore and Parcy Moore 99
Section III Part A Abner Keyes and Civy I Moore /Maggie Jones 100
Section III Part B Generation 4 Annie Keyes and
        Sylvester Washington 100
Section III Part C Margie Keyes and John Smith.................................. 101
Section IV Philip Keyes/ Elizabeth (Bessie) Keyes/Lizzie Kennedy 101
Section V Part A Harriet Keyes and Nelson Pender............................ 101
Section VI Part A Josephus Keyes and Elizabeth Moore..................... 102
Section VI Part B Virginia Keyes and James M Moore 102
Section VI Part C Veva Keyes.. 102
Section VI Part D Murphy Keyes and Anna L Peacock........................ 103
Section VII Part A Graham Keyes and Carrie Sutton 103
Section VIII Part A Romey Keyes Thelma Green 104
Section IX Part A Julia Keyes / Joseph Stilley/John Murray 104
Section X Part A Tiny Keyes and Josephine Minor 104
Section X Part B Leon Keyes and Emily Wright................................... 105
Section X Part C Mary A Keyes and Clifford O Moore 105
Section X Part D Oswald Keyes and Eileen/Fanny/Carrie 106

Section X Part E Eula V Keyes and John Leslie Moore 106
Section X Part F Francis Marie Keyes and Louis Seville 106
Section X Part G Selma Keyes and Leatha O Gaye 107
Section X Part H Burnic Keyes and Mary A McCary 107
Section X Part I Lena B Keyes and Henry Myers 107

Chapter 8

Section I 108
Section II 120

Reference 151

Foreword

Over 225 years of Keys/Keyes in Eastern North Carolina by Bunyon Keys, a native son of Blounts Creek offers the readers an insight of the Keys Families that originated in Blounts Creek, Beaufort County and spread not only to Eastern North Carolina, but throughout many parts of the United States and several other areas of the world. Listed in many documents, I have seen the name spelled as Keys, Kee, Key, Keyes, Kees, Keais, Keen and many other variations. Taken from the "Surname Data Base Last Name Origin" from the internet; The surname Keys is English and was first recorded as belonging to the family of Roger Keys. The recorded information was dated 1275. For simplicity, I have in most cases used the spelling Keys or Keyes. The Keys (families) were started by Milley Keys, except for one family in this area and that family is listed in Chapter 7 of this document. There are some instances where the two families inter-married. The 2nd family was the decedents of William Keys from Virginia perhaps a cousin of Milley. (Evidence points to Milley's ancestors being from England and dating back to the mid 1650's.)

I couldn't find any evidence pointing to a husband for Milley. According to Article XIV of the North Carolina Constitution stated that "Marriage between one man and one woman is the only domestic legal union that shall be valid or recognized in this State." Article XIV was amended by Chapter XXX which stated "An Ordnance to Amend Article Fourteen of the Constitution, Prohibiting Intermarriage of the Races...' was adopted on the 11th day of October, A.D. 1875.

According to the law of the land at that time, Milley could have taken any man she wanted as a husband and may have taken a slave as husband. This was not uncommon, I have found evidence that many Free Persons of Color (Black People) took slaves as their spouses. The status of a child was dependent on the status of the mother, i.e., if the mother was a slave, the child would be a slave and if the mother was a Free Person of Color, the child would be free.

The Keys' were a large family, second only to the Moor's that originated in Blounts Creek. I published a Book, "*Over Three Hundred Years Of Black People in Blounts Creek, Beaufort County North Carolina, Book 1*" in 2014. In some instances, I will make references to the above Book as just *Book I*. In *Book I*, I promised my readers that there would be a Book 2; **This is not Book 2**. Some information that is contained in this Book may be included or expanded on in Book 2, however, this Book is published to show the degree and influence the Keys Families had within this and surrounding areas without being obscured by the Moor Families. It is not a prerequisite to read *Book I* prior reading this Book, however, it would help.

There was a law in North Carolina that had a great effect on many families in North Carolina and is described as follows: <u>Chapter 5, section 1 and 5 of the Revised Statues of the State of North Carolina passed by the General Assembly at the Section of 1836-7...(Raleigh: Turner and Hughes, 1837</u> is quoted in part:

"...the courts of pleas and quarter sessions had the authority "to bind out, as apprentices, all orphans whose estates are of so small value that no person will educate and maintain him or her for the profits thereof; also all children under age whose fathers have deserted their families, and have been absent for the term of one year, leaving them without sufficient support, or where application may be made to the wardens of the poor for relief...also all free base born children." The law continued, "The court of pleas and quarter sessions shall likewise have power...to bind out as apprentices all free base born children of color, and all the children of free negroes and mulattoes where the parents with whom such children may live, do or shall not habitually employ his or her time in some honest, industrious occupations...Males were usually bound until the age of 21, while females were bound until they were 18, except females of color, who were bound until them, too, reached 21. The master was to provide his apprentice "diet, clothes, lodging, and accommodations fit and necessary, and shall teach and cause him or her to be taught to read and write...it shall not be incumbent upon the master of a colored apprentice to teach him or her to read and write." Upon the expiration of the apprenticeship, the master was to provide the apprentice with $6, a new suit of clothes, and a new Bible." Base on this law, many families had to appear in the court system for their children to be bonded out as apprentices.

This law seems to have a two part effect: (1) A family could have several children and if they fell within the purview described above, the systems would intervene and supposedly take care of the children and (2) the law provided certain people, especially those with a degree of social status, a way to get work done basically free by assigning these children to work for a fixed number of years as apprentices.

Sometimes a man, who had an outside (bastard) child and had a certain amount of social status and with the collusion of an affluent person, could get that child assigned to himself as apprentices. So was the case with some of Milley's decedents.

Much of the information about Milley's family was taken from the U.S. Census. Prior to the 1850 U.S. Census, only the head of household was listed by name. The other member(s) were listed as follows: "other free" or "other free persons". Two examples are provided below:

Nancy Keys, the daughters of Milly Keys, was born about 1771. She was head of a household with four free persons in 1810; two males born before 1806 and one female born before 1806.

Charity Keys, (Clary), the daughter of Milly Keys, was born about 1776. She was head of household with five other free in 1810."

xvii

When I could find the age of one of Milley's decedents, I would take that age and compare it with one of the examples above to determine the parent of that decedent.

Chapter 8 contains Family Tree Charts for Kee, Milley's and many of Milley's decedents.

Chapter 1
Section I
Part A
Overview

Paul Heinegg, in his Book, *Free African Americans of North Carolina, Virginia, and South Carolina* from the Colonial period to about 1820; Fifth Edition, provided a wealth of information about Free People of Color (Black People) in this area. Some of these Black People were the Moors, Blango and Keys. For simplicity, I have in most cases; use the spelling Keys or Keyes. Heinegg first spelling was Kee. Kee, no first name, was born in 1700 and was a soldier who was slain in the expedition against the Spaniards at Cartagena.

Richard Hayes Phillips, Ph.D. in his Book, White Slave Children of Colonial Maryland and Virginia: Birth and Shipping Records stated in part "that there was a law dated 1659 in the Country of England… that authorized constables to kidnap children found begging and vagrant had the effect of allowing ship captain and sailors to sprint away children, who were available for the taking…these children were bought to the Colonies of Virginia and Maryland and sold into slavery. The author went on to stat that "These children were to serve a fix number of years set by the court…; [and] five thousands kids were captured and sold into slavery…" under this law. It seems that most of the children were release on or before their 24th birthday unless they had additional time added on because of some type of infraction.

In Phillips's Book the following recording of "Key Thomas, son of Thomas and Mary Key, Born 17 January 1663, Baptized 21 January 1663, Saint James, Colchester, Essex, England. [The 2nd recording] Key, Thomas, 20 June 1676, age 15, Talbot County, Maryland,

Edward Elliote, seven years". What is stated here is there was a boy, Thomas, the son of Thomas and Mary Key of England who was captured and sold in to slavery. At the age of 15, he was in the household of Edward Elliote, Talbot County, Maryland with seven more years to serve. Perhaps after his release he left the Maryland Colony and moved to the Virginia Colony. Thomas could have been the father of Kee, mentioned above.

According to the Wikipedia, The Free Encyclopedia; Cartagena is a city of the Indies and is located on the northern cost of Colombia in the Caribbean Coastal Region. In March 1741, the city was invaded by a large force of British and American colonial troops. The invading forces consisted of 23,600 men. After weeks of fighting the siege was broken off due to the start of the tropical rainy season and many of the invading troops came down with diseases such as the yellow fever. (In short the invading force lost the battle.) Heinegg further states that Kee's wife, Elizabeth Kee was granted an allowance of five pounds on 26 May 1742 for Kee's military service. Elizabeth is described as a "Mulatto", (a light skin person.) Kee and his wife, Elizabeth were the ancestors of many families including Milley Keys of Beaufort County. (In different documents, including the Old World Tree, I have seen Milley as being born in 175? [No year], 1750 and 1765. Observing the age of her children, I am inclined to believe that she was born before 1760 and arrived in Blounts Creek before 1775.

Section II
Part A
Milley's Children

According to Paul Heinegg's, Book: *Free African Americans of North Carolina, Virginia, and South Carolina, Volume II:* and many of the U.S. Census, Milley was born about 1760, in 1790 U.S. Census she had three children living with her. Evidence indicates that she had 11 children and many of her children were born before 1790. They could have been living in someone else's household when the Census was taken. I, the author, am in the seventh generation of Milley's family. Perhaps Milley didn't know Keziah Moore, "*Book I, Chapter III*", but she probably knew Keziah's granddaughter, Lucy. At least two of Lucy's sons, Willoughby and Giles married, or had children by at least four of Milley's daughters or granddaughters. Also, at least one of Lucy's great granddaughters married a grandson of Milley. I, (the author), am in the six generation of Lucy's family. In different documents, there were many different spelling for Milley' name.

Milley's Children were:

1. Amy, born about 1769; (see Sec II Part B, below, this document.)
2. Nancy, born about 1771; (sec II, Part C, below, this document.)
3. Sally, born about 1773, (Chapter 2, this document.)
4. William, born about 1774, (Chapter 3, this document; Gentleman Giles Moore, Lydia, Grace and Mary Ann, the daughters of William; are also in Chapter 4.)
5. Clary, (Charity) born about 1776 ;(Sec II Part D)
6. Lucy, born about 1775 ;(Section II, Part E)
7. Silvy, born about 1780; (Section II, Part F)
8. Wyatt, born in 1780; (Section II Part G)
9. Malachi Keys was born about 1784; (Section II, Part H)
10. Penny, born about 1786; (I can't find any evidence that Penny had any children.)
11. Milley, born about 1790, (Chapter 4, this document)
12. Mary, born about 1793; (Chapters 5 and 6, this document)

Miley owned property in Blounts Creek, North Carolina. In the 1790 Tax Records, she paid taxes on land in Beaufort County, N.C.

Section II
Part B
Amy Keys and Willoughby Moore

Amy Keys, the daughter of Milly Keys, was born about 1769. She was the head of a household of two other free in 1810. These other two free people, in all probability, were her husband Willoughby and her daughter Mary. Willoughby, born about 1769, was the son of John Moore and the step son of Lucy Moore. Willoughby made a will dated 25th day of August 1823, where he left his wife Amy 50 acres of land and the rest to his daughter, Mary. (For more information See *Book I, Chapter 3, Section II, Part D*.) In the 1850 U.S. Census, Amy, at the age of 81, is in the household of Giles Moore. Giles is listed as being 103 years old. Giles may have been kin to Willoughby. Also listed is a girl name Theresa Green, age 4.

Section II
Part C
Nancy Keys

Nancy Keys, the daughters of Milly Keys, was born about 1771. She was head of a household with four free persons in 1810; two males born before 1806 and one female born before 1806. One of the males could have been Southey Keys, born in 1805.

Section II
Part C-2
Southey Keys

Southey Keys, the son of Milley was born in 1805. In the 1840 U.S. Census, he is listed as Head of household with five other Free Colored Persons (a total of 6): (1) Himself, between the ages of 24-35; (2), his wife, between the ages of 24-35; (3), One male between the ages of 10-23, (perhaps this Southey that died in 1881, (this Southey did not have any heirs); (4), one female under the age of ten; (5), One male under the age of 10 and (6) one female between the ages of 10-23. This female could have been Sara, (aka Sara Frances, aka Fanny Stilley, aka Amanda born September 7, 1826 and died October 14, 1907 ;)

Section II
Part C-3
Sara Keys and March Stilley

Sara married March Stilley, my 3rd Great- grandfather. March was born in 1794 and died September 18, 1883.

The following extract was taken from the Beaufort County Marriage Records (1851-1866) "March Stilley, a freeman appeared before me the 6th day of August 1866 for himself and as the next friend and [attorney] of Fanny Keas who say that they have been cohabiting together as husband and wife for 23 years and desire so now by mutual consent."

Prior to 1865, March was a slave and Sara was free. They cohabited because they could not legally get married. Slaves were allowed to court during their "free time". They were also allowed to go to other farms (plantations) as long as they returned home when they were supposed to. March and Sara started courting in 1843, 22 years before the Civil War ended.

March had a son, March (Jr) born in 1838 who was not listed as Sara's son. (There is no record for the mother of March Jr. This March was my 2nd Great Grandfather.)

March and Sara had five children: (1) Zachariah born September 8, 1848 and died January 8, 1923; (2) Lewis J born March 9, 1850 and died July 29, 1923; (3) Olivia born March 17, 1851 and died January 17, 1918; (4) Frank born 1850 and died September 6, 1929 and (5) Mary Martha born September 11, 1866 and died April 1, 1914.

Section II
Part C-3-2
Zachariah (Zach) Stilley and Lydia Ann Moore

Zach Stilley, son of March Stilley and Sara Keyes, was born September 11, 1848. He died January 8, 1923. In the 1910 United States Census, he is married to Lydia Ann Moore. Lydia was the daughter of Israel and Mary Moore. She was born in 1871. Zach Stilley and Lydia Moore had three children: (1) Siddie born 1903; (2) Laurie born 1904 and (3) Ann born 1904. Zach and his family lived in the Bonnerton Community of Beaufort County.

Section II
Part C-3-3
Lewis Johnson Stilley and Henrietta Pike

Lewis J Stilley, son of March Stilley and Sara Keyes, was born March 9, 1850 and died July 29, 1923. He married Henriette Pike in 1883. Henrietta was born in March 1855 and died May 4, 1925. Her parents were Jeffery Pike and Violet Pritchett. Lewis and Henrietta Pike Stilley had nine children (1) Frank, born in 1885; (2) Minnie, born in 1888; (3) Blanch, born in 1890; (4) Hiram, born in 1893; (5) Eugene, born in 1895; (6) Julia, born in 1897; (7) Carrie, born in 1898; (8) Isaac, born in 1898 and (9) Ethel, born in 1903.

Section II
Part C-3-4
Olivia Stilley and Stephen Little

Olivia Stilley, daughter of March Stilley and Sara Keys, was born March 17, 1851 and died January 17, 1918. She married Stephen Little, son of Rhoden Little and Sara Smallwood. Prior to his marriage to Olivia, Stephen was married to Ruth (Jr.) Tripp, the daughter of Ruth (Sr.) Tripp was born in 1825. Ruth was born in 1882. Stephen and Ruth had 11 children: (1) Siddie born 1882; (2)

Aaron born 1885; (3) Ella born 1887; (4) Luvenia born 1889; (5) James H. Born 1891; (6) Roden born 1893; (7) Beda born 1895; (8) Joseph born 1897; (9) Sallie born 1898; (10) Ruth born 1902 and (11) Gertrude born 1905. In the 1910 United States Census, Olivia Stilley and Stephen Little are married and six of Stephen children from his previous marriage to Ruth are living with them. In the 1920 United States Census, there are four children listed for Olivia and Stephen: (1) Emma born 1911; (2) Rumley born 1914; (3) Stephen born 1915 and (4) Maggie born 1918. Olivia and Stephen resided in the Edward Community of Beaufort County.

Section II
Part C-3-5
Frank Stilley

Frank Stilley, son of March Stilley and Sara Keys, was born in 1850 and died September 6, 1929. His death Certificate indicated that he had never been married and there is no evidence that he ever had any children.

Section II
Part C-3-6
Mary Stilley and James Gardner

Mary Stilley, daughter of March Stilley and Sara Keys was born September 11, 1866 and died April 1, 1914. She married James Gardner of Aurora, North Carolina. James was born in 1854. Mary and James had six children: (1) William, born in 1881; (2) Laura P, born in 1882; (3) James C, born in 1893; (4) William A, born in 1898 and (5) Gardner born in 1900 and (6) (no names) that was also born in 1900.

As stated above, Southey, the brother of Sara, that died in 1881 did not have any heirs. He left his land to the children of his sister, Sara. There was a State of North Carolina, Beaufort County Document dated 23rd day of March AD, 1907 where all of March and Sara's children (name listed in the above paragraphs) agreed to sell the land left to them by their uncle, Suthy (Southey) Keise (Keys).

Section II
Part D
Charity (Clary) Keys

Charity Keys, (Clary), the daughter of Milly Keys, was born about 1776. She was head of household with five other free in 1810. One of these free people could have been named Noah. At the age of 74, in the 1850 U.S. Census she is living in Morven, Anson, North Carolina with Noah Keys, born in 1815 as head of household. ; Also living in the same household were Sara Keys, born in 1808 and Lydia Keys, born in 1806. There was another lady named Mary Keys, born in 1812 and died in 1870 were Noah, Sara and Lydia's sister. Mary Keys must have married Dove Teal because her last name is listed as Teal in the 1850 U.S. Census.

Listed in the 1850 U.S. Census, was Mary Teal, age 38, as head of household, William Teal, age 15, Noah Teal, age 13, Elle Teal, age 9 and Benjamin teal, age 4. Some of their sister, Mary's, children, were living with them.

In the 1860 U.S. Census, Lydia Keys, age 54, is listed as head of household. Addition to the household is Sara Keys, age 52; Noah Keys, age 46; Ellen Teal, age 16 and Benjamin, age 14.

Section II
Part E
Lucy Keys

Lucy Keys, the daughter of Miley Keys, was born about 1775. In the 1860 U.S. Census, she is living in District 1, Martin County, North Carolina with the following children: (1) John,(son) born in 1813;

(2) Fanney, (daughter) born in 1830 and two grandchildren born in 1853 and 1855. Fanny was listed as her daughter but because of the difference of their ages, Fanny may have been her granddaughter and may have been the mother of the two other children.

Section II
Part E-2
John Keys and Emerline Grice

John Keys, the son of Lucy Keys, was born in 1813. He married Emerline Grice. Emerline was born in in 1836. John Keys and Emerline Grice Keys had a child, William Keys, born in 1856.

Section II
Part E-2-2
William Keys and Evalina E Hunter

William Keys, the son of John and Emerline Grice Keys, was born January 15, 1856 and died June 30, 1926. He married Evalina Ester Hunter, the daughter of Henry (born in 1815) and Evalina Hunter. Evalina was born December 10, 1853 and died January 2, 1915. William and Evalina lived in the Keysville area of Beaufort County. William and Evalina E Hunter Keys had the following children: (1) Dollie A, born in 1880; (2) William A, born in 1881; (3) Della B, born in 1887; (4) David R, born in 1889; (In the 1940 U.S. Census, David is living in Washington, D.C.) and (5) Mutter, born in 1892.

Section II
Part E-2-2-2
Della Keys and Joseph Payton

Della Keys, the daughter of William and Evalina E Hunter Keys, was born April 22, 1886 and died June 4, 1951. She married Joseph Payton on March 17, 1909. Joseph was born in 1887. Joseph and

Della Keys Payton had at least two children: (1) William A, born in 1910 and (2) Austin, born in 1912.

Section II
Part F
Silvy (Sebry) Keys

Silvy (Sebry) Keys, the daughter of Milly Keys, was born about 1780. She was head of household with two other free in 1810. One of the free was her son Zachariah born in 1834. In the 1860 U.S Census, at the age of 80, Silvy was living in Washington, Beaufort County, North Carolina with the following members in her household: (1) Zach, born in 1814; (2) Mary, (Zack wife) born in 1832; (3) William, born in 1838; (4) Ruther, born in 1940; (5) Octavia, born in 1856 and (5) Elizabeth, born in 1859. Because of the closeness of the ages of William, Ruther and Mary, William and Ruther may have been Zack's children by another woman.

Section II
Part F-2
Zack Keys and Mary Keys

Zack Keys the son of Silvy Keys was born in 1814. In the 1860 U.S. Census, Zack is married to a lady named Mary, born in 1832. Zack's, mother, Silvy, is also living in his household at the age of 80. Zack and Mary Keys had seven children: (1) Octavia, born in 1856; (2) Elizabeth, born in 1859; (3) Zachariah Jr., born in 1861; (4) Mary P, born in 1865; (5) James H, born in 1867; (6) Eddie, born in 1869 and (7) Annie S, born in 1874. Zack's and Mary's first three children were born in Beaufort County, North Carolina and the other were born in Camden, New Haven, Connecticut

Section II
Part G
Wyatt Keys (Keas) and Jeliky Rhodes

Wyatt Keys, the son of Milley Keys, was born in 1780. He married Jeliky Rhodes on June 14, 1832 in Craven County, North Carolina. In the 1830 U.S. Census, Wyatt is living in Jameston [Jamestown), Martin [County], North Carolina with a total of five persons in his household; one male between the ages of 36-54; one female between the ages of 36-54 and three slaves women 100 years and over. In the 1850 U.S. Census, Wyatt is 70 years old and is living in the household with Thomas Buttery [Bundy], age 45, his wife Rachel, age 45 and two children Mary I, age 20 and Thomas, age 11. Also living in the dwelling are two ladies, Lucy Barley, age 55 and Susan Keys, age 18.

Section II
Part H
Malachi Keys

Malachi Keys, the son of Milly Keys, was born in 1784. In the 1840 U.S. Census, he is living in Williamston, Martin County, North Carolina. He had one son, perhaps Malachi born about 1810.

Section II
Part H-2
Malachi (Maliki) Keys and Penny Keys/Nelly Keys

Malachi Keys, the son of Malachi Keys, was born about 1810. In the 1850 U.S. Census he was married to Penny Keys. Penny was born in 1811. Malachi and Penny Keys had five children: (1) Azariah, born in 1839; (2) Patsey, born in 1844; (3) Elizabeth, born in 1846; (4) Nibkak, born in 1849 and (5) Maliki, born in 1842.

In the 1870 U.S. Census, Malachi is married to Nelly Keys. Nelly was born in 1825. Malachi and Nelly Keys had seven children: (1) Eliza, born in 1851, (2) Lucy, born in 1858; (3) Deller, born in 1861; (4) Elizabeth, born in 1863; (5) Asa, born in 1867; (6) William H, born in 1869 and (7) Nancy, born in 1867.

Nelly had a daughter, B.E. (no name listed), born in 1852 prior to marring Malachi; in the 1880 U.S. Census, B.E. is living with them and is listed as Malachi's step-daughter. B.E. had the following children: (1) Henry, born in 1868; (2) Emma, born in 1871; (3) George, born in 1874; (4) Louisa, born in 1875; (5) Nicey, born in 1876 and (6)Johnny, born in 1879. (B.E. and all of her children went in the last name Keys.

Chapter 2
Section I
Part A
Sally Keys

Sally Keys, the daughter of Milley was, born about 1773. She is listed as head of a Beaufort County household with 5 free in 1820. One of those children could have been John born in 1796.

Section II
Part A
John Keys and Mary Keys

John Keys, the son of Sally Keys, was born in 1796. In the 1850 U.S. Census he is married to Mary Keys. Mary was born in 1812. John and Mary had seven children: (1) Kennedy, born in 1832; (2) John (Jr.), born in 1834; (3) Pheraby, born in 1836; (4) William, born in 1837; (5) David, born in 1839; (6) Joseph, born in 1841 and (7) Isiah, born in 1843.

Section II
Part B
John Jr. Keys and Nancy Keys

John Jr. Keys, the son of John and Mary Keys, was born in 1834. He married Nancy (last name unknown). John Jr. and Nancy Keys had two children: (1) Mary, born in 1854 and (2) Bannon, born in 1857.

Section III
Part A
1st Bannon Keyes and Peggy a Moore
(There were two Bannon and Peggy)

Bannon Keys, the son of John and Nancy Kees/Keys, was born in 1857. He married Peggy A Moore (my, the author great aunt), daughter of Gilles and Lucy Moore. Peggy was born in 1865 and died in 1944. Bannon and Peggy Moore Keys had five children: (1) Lacy, born in 1901 and died December 24, 1937; (2) Sussie (Suzzy), born June 18, 1907 and died November 1986; (3) Simon, born in 1911 and died December 14, 1957; (4) David (never married), born March 10, 1900 and died December 14, 1957; (5) Tinsey, born 1902

Section III
Part B
Lacy Keyes and Estelle Williams

Lacy Keyes, son of Bannon and Peggy A Moore Keyes, was born in, born in 1901 and died December 24, 1937. Lacy married Estelle Williams, daughter of John R and Mattie Carter Williams. Estelle was born February 8, 1902 and died September 1980. Lacy and Estelle Williams Keyes had 10 children: (1) Gus, born in 1919; (2) Peggy, born in 1924; (3) John E, born in 1928; (4) Mattie R, born in 1930 (married Linwood Martin); (5) Felbert was born November 13, 1931 and died April 23, 1988. (On Filbert's Death certificated, he was listed as being single ;) (6) Doris, born in 1934; (7) Mary, born in 1935 ; (8) Robert (Buddy), born in March 30, 1937 and died February 7, 1995 in New Bern North Carolina; (9) Estelle Eula (Sissy), born in 1939 and died July 8, 1977. On her Death Certificate, she is listed as being single; never married and (10) Troy.

Section III
Part B-2
Gus Keyes and Hansel L Moore

Gus Keyes, son of Lacy and Estella Williams Keyes, was born December 15, 1919 and died December 22, 1980. He married Hansel L Moore, daughter of Nicia and Jessie L Moore. Hansel was born February 13, 1922 and died June 28, 2005. Gus and Hansel L

Moore had seven children: (1) Shelly, born in 1943; (2) William E, born September 15, 1945; (3) Leola; (4) Beatrice, born November 6, 1950; (5) Chester, born May 17, 1953 and died in 2018; (6) Malvin A, born May 7, 1952 and (7) Rayvon, born May 30, 1954. At the time of her death, Hansel had 36 grandchildren, 44 great grandchildren and one great-great grandchild.

Section III
Part B-3
Peggy Keyes and John Harold Peterson

Peggy Keyes, daughter of Lacy and Estella Williams Keyes, was born January 15, 1924 and died December 10, 2004. She married John H Peterson on September 19, 1950. John was the son of Charles and Lavinia Peterson. John was born in Swan Quarters, Hyde County, North Carolina in 1920 and died September 5, 1968. Peggy had two children who went in the last name of Keyes. They were, (1) David E, born September 9, 1964 and (2) Tyrone, born August 17, 1965.

Section III
Part B-4
John Earl Keyes and Lizena O'Neal

John E Keyes, son of Lacy and Estella Williams Keyes, was born in 1928 and died June 26, 1997. He married Lizena O'Neal on May 20, 1951. Lizena was the daughter of Orlanda and Annie O'Neal. Lizena was born November 10, 1932 in Hyde County, North Carolina.

Section III
Part B-5
Mattie R Keyes and Linwood Martin

Mattie Keyes, daughter of Lacy and Estella Williams Keyes, was born in 1930. She married Linwood Martin, son of Linwood and Sara

Ann Carter Martin. Linwood was born February 15, 1907 and died September 17, 1973.

Section III
Part B-6
Doris Keyes and Thomas Jr. Myer

Doris Keys, daughter of Lacy and Estella Williams Keyes, was born August 10, 1934 and died March 19, 2007. She married Tomas Jr. Myers, son of Thomas and Emmeline Myers. Thomas was born in 1904 and died September 12, 1982. Doris had six children and evidence points to the children being born before she married Thomas. The children were: (1) Edward L, born June 21, 1953; (2) James A, born January 31, 1958; (3) Lee T, born October 27, 1952; (4) Brenda F, born November 23, 1950; (5) Cynthia, born March 4, 1952 and (6) Rebecca, born March 20, 1956 and died December 8, 1959. On Rebecca's Death Certificate, James Carter is listed as her father. (For more information about Thomas Jr. Myers, see Chapter 1, Section II, Part B-2-3 this document.)

When Doris passed, she had the following direct decedents listed on her Obituary: (1) Lacey L Keyes; (2) Wanda German (Milton); (3) Jimmie Keyes (Shamika); (4) Michelle Best (Rodney); (5) Lahonda Waltower; (6) Wilhelmina Waltower; (7) Brenda K Waltower; (8) Arthur Waltower, Jr,; (9) Travis Waltower: (10) Edward Keyes; (11) Doris Keyes; (12) Lakeisha Keyes; (13) Kizzy Keyes; (14) Edward Keyes Jr.; (15) Katrina Willis (Dawan); (16) Sinetta Keyes; (17) Ronetta Cariaga (Laroyce), (18) Shanquetta Keyes. (Doris had 33 great grandchildren and one great-great grandchild.)

Section III
Part C
Tinsey Keyes and Leroy Moore

Tinsey Keyes, daughter of Bannon and Peggy A Moore Keyes, was born April 11, 1902 and died February 9, 1987. She married Leroy Moore. Leroy was born in Beaufort County November 22, 1896 and died September 3, 1938 in Beaufort County. Leroy served in the U.S. Army. Leroy and Tinsey Keyes Moore had one son, Troy L Moore. Troy was born May 11, 1926 and died January 18, 2003. Troy also served in the U.S. Army.

Section III
Part D
Southey (Susie) (Suzzy) Keyes and Betty/Lillian/Jasper Smith

Suzzy Keyes, son of Bannon and Peggy A Moore Keyes, was born July 18, 1907 and died November 1986. He married Bettie E Moore on April 6, 1929. Bettie was the daughter of John Abe and Martha Moore of the Bonnerton Community of Beaufort County, North Carolina. Bettie was born on February 13, 1913 and died February 5, 1950. Sometime after Bettie died, Suzzy married Lillian. Suzzy and his wives had the 14 children: (1) Giles, born December 29, 1934 and died April 15, 1999; (2) Suzzy Jr., born December 3, 1936; (3) Fred, born June 18, 1939; (4) John Ed, born February 26, 1943; (5) Jack, born January 20, 1942 and died March 28, 1942; (6) Richard; (7) Carlton, born 1954; (8) Alonza; (9) Joseph (Ricky); (10) Helen, born January 2, 1945; (11) Betty; (12) Pearl; (13) Jessie and (14) Nellie. Nellie married Willie Carter.

Section III
Part E
Simon (Booth) Keyes and Maggie Moore

Simon Keyes, son of Bannon and Peggy Moore, was born September 2, 1912 and died October 21, 1964. He married Maggie Moore, daughter of John A and Martha Moore, of the Bonnerton Community of Beaufort County, North Carolina. Maggie was born June 22, 1919 and died December 15, 1965; Simon and Maggie Moore Keyes had nine children: (1) Peggy; (2) Emma, born in 1937; (3) Hattie, born September 28, 1940; (4) Graddy (Pie); (5) Simon, born May 3, 1938 and died January 8, 1984. (According to information contained on his Death Certificate, he was never married); (6) Phyllis; (7) Albert; (8) Rowena and (9) John David, born February 14, 1945 and died April 8, 1959. (According to information contained on his Death he was never married.)

Section IV
Part A
Isaiah Keys and Freddia A Moore/Peggy Moore

Isaiah Keys, the son of John and Mary Keys, was born in 1843 and died in 1914. He married Freddia Moore. Isaiah and Freddia A. Moore Keys had one daughter, Fevby born in 1863. Freddia died and Isaiah married Peggy Moore the widow of James Moore. After Isaiah and Peggy were married, two of Peggy's children, Israel and Margaret and Isaiah's daughter, Fevby, lived with them.

Israel Albert Moore, son of Peggy and James Moore, was born in 1862 and died March 22, 1931. While living in the household of Isaiah and Peggy, Israel and Fevby had three daughters; (Israel and Fevby never married). The daughters were: (1) Mamie Keys, born in 1891 and died November 16, 1961; (2) Melisa Keys, born in 1885 and (3) Sallie Keys, born 1889. (Israel daughters are listed in *Book One, Chapter IV, Section V, Part A.*)

Section IV
Part B
Fevby (Ferraby) Keys and Alonzo Blango

Fevby Keys, the daughter Isaiah and Freddia Keys, was born in 1863 and died April 9, 1920. She married Alonzo Blango, the son of Phebe Blango. He was born in 1874. It seems that for a while Alonzo went as Alonzo Moore. In the 1900 U.S. Census, he is Alonzo Moore, married to Ferraby Keyes. In the 1910 U.S. Census he is listed as Alonzo Blango and married to Fevby with two children: (1) Elijah, born in 1896 and (2) Angeline (Lina), born in 1899; (The family of Fevby and Alonzo Blango is listed in *Book One, Chapter V, Section IV.)*

Chapter 3
Section I
Part A
William Keys and Mary Thornton

William Keys, the son of Milly Keys, was born about 1774. He married Mary Thornton on December 3, 1825. They had four children: (1) Lydia, born 1805; (2) Grace, born in 1820; (3) Mary Ann Green, born in 1821. (Mary may have been their half- sister because of her last name) and (4) William Keys Jr., also born in 1821.

Lydia, Grace and Mary formed a quasi-polygamy family among themselves. This arraignment must have taken place prior to 1841, the year that Mary's, son, Henry was born. The arraignment was polygamy because all three ladies had children by the same man and quasi-polygamy because all of them didn't live in the same household. Lydia and Giles had four children: (1) Martha P, born in 1830; (2) Mary, born in 1831; (3) William P, born in 1837 and (4) John, born in 1842. Giles and Grace had three children: (1) Elizabeth, born in 1840 and died in 1857; (2) James, born in 1843 and (3) Mary Jean, born in 1853.

Mary and Giles had one child, Henry, born in 1842. Henry moved to Washington, Beaufort County, North Carolina as a young man. (There is no other information available about Henry at this time.)

(Note: Perhaps Lydia and her siblings accepted this type of arrangement because they came from a household where all of the children didn't seem to have the same parents.)

Section II
Part A
Lydia Keys and Giles (Gent Giles) Moore

Lydia Keys, the daughter of William and Mary Thornton Moore, was born in 1810 and died before 1870. She married Gentleman Giles Moore, son of Lucy Moore and John Moore. He was born about 1792 and died before 1860. Giles and Lydia Keys Moore had four children: (1) Martha Peggy (went by her middle name Peggy), born in 1830 (2) Mary born in 1831; (3) William Plas (went by his middle name Plas) born in 1837 and (4) John, born in 1842.

Section II
Part B
Descendants of Peggy Moore and James H Moore/Isaiah Keys

Peggy Moore, the daughter of Gentleman Giles Moore and Lydia Keys Moore, was born in 1831 and died before 1915. She married James H Moore. He was born in 1826 and died about 1867. After Peggy got married, she and her husband, James, lived with her mother, Lydia (Ma Lydia). James served in the Civil War. James H. Moore and Peggy Moore had four children: (1) William Riley (went by the name Riley) was born in 1854; (2) Edward, born in 1856; (3) Israel A. born in 1862 and (4) Margaret born in 1865.

After James died, Peggy Married Isaiah Keys, born in 1838 and died in 1914. Isaiah's parents were John Keys and Mary Keys. Isaiah's first wife was Freddia Moore. Isaiah and Freddia had one daughter, Fevby born in 1863. After Isaiah and Peggy got married, two of Peggy's children, Israel and Margaret and Isaiah's daughter, Fevby, lived with them.

Section II
Part C
Mary Moore and Israel Moore

Mary Moore, the daughter of Gentleman Giles Moore and Lydia Keys Moore, was born 1831. She married Israel Moore. Israel was born in 1833, Mary and Israel Moore had three children: (1) Lydia, born in 1871. She married Zach Stilley, (Chapter 1, Section II, Part C-3-2 above; (2) Henry, born in 1876 and (3) William, born in 1879.

Section II
Part D
William Plas and Sara Ann Lindsey

William P Moore (went by his middle name Plas), the son of Gentleman Giles Moore and Lydia Keys Moore, was born in 1837. He married Sara Lindsey. He also had at least two children by a woman named, Lydia Moore. Plas had eight children, they were: (1) William Henry (dropped his first name William, and went by the name, Henry Plas, by Sara. Henry was born February 18, 1882 in Blounts Creek and died June 30, 1953 in Suffolk, Nansemond, Virginia. (2) Nancy, by Sara, born in 1892 and died September 17, 1915; (3) Noah, born in 1892, (Noah and Nancy must have been twins; (4) Worstey (Vaster), born in 1885 and died in 1923, by Lydia; (5) Miney, born in 1900; (6) Pearlie, born in 1901 and died in 1994, by Lydia; (7) Tiny, born in 1904, by Sara and (8) Joshua, born in 1907, by Sara.

Section II
Part D-2
Henry Moore and Della Aldridge

Henry Moore, the son of William Plas and Sara, was born February 18, 1882 in Blounts Creek, North Carolina and died June 30, 1953 in Suffolk, Nansemond, Virginia. He married Della Aldridge, daughter of Henry Aldridge and Sara Gaskill Aldridge. Della was born April 18, 1886 in Blounts Creek, North Carolina and died July 31, 1954 in Norfolk, Virginia. Children of Della Aldridge Moore and Henry P Moore were: (1) Beulah, born in 1914; (2) Roosevelt, born in 1915; (3) Callonia, born in 1911 and (4) Allen born in 1906. *(Note: Henry had a son, Mack H Moore. Mack was born 1890 and died October 20, 1973, by Lucy Moore, daughter of John G and Ann Moore before he married Della.)*

Henry separated from Della and moved to Virginia where he raised another family. According to the 1940 U.S. Census, Henry was living in Winsor, Isle of Wright, Virginia. He was married to Marrie and they had six children: (1) Percell born in 1922; (2) Robert born in 1924; (3) Simma born in 1926; (4) Marrie born in 1928; (5) James Russell born in 1928 and (6) Henry born in 1934.

Section II

Part D-2-2

Roosevelt Moore and Melvina Moore

Roosevelt Moore, son of Della Aldridge Moore and Henry P Moore, was born in February 28, 1917 and died January 25, 1985. He married Melvina Hill, daughter of Edward Hill and Serena Moore Hill. Melvina was born August 8, 1919 and died December 6, 1996. Roosevelt had one daughter, Sina prior to his marriage to Melvina. Sina mother was Inez. Roosevelt Moore and Melvina Hill Moore had fourteen children: (1) Madelyn; (2) Erma L; (3) Roosevelt Jr.; (4) Edd M; (5) Wilhelmina; (6) Dupree L; (7) Delphia L; (8) Carl U; (9) Alphonza; (10) Lloyd V; (11) Juattee; (12) Della; (13) Diane and (14) Edmond J.

Section II
Part D-2-3
Noah E Moore and Jennie Moore

Noah, son of William Plas and Sara was born in 1893 in Blounts Creek and died February 15, 1970 in New Bern, Craven County, North Carolina. He married Jennie Crawford, daughter of Major Crawford and Josephine King. Jennie was born February 25, 1899 and died July 5, 1995 in Washington, North Carolina. In the 1940 U.S. Census, Noah and Jennie were living in Chocowinity, Beaufort County, North Carolina. Living with them was Noah sister, Minnie born in 1901. (She was listed as a widow.)

Section II
Part D-2-4
Worstey (Vaster) Moore and Major Birt

Worstey Moore, daughter of Henry P Moore and Lydia Moore, was born in 1885 and died in 1923. She married Major Birt, son of Matilda (Tillda) Birt and William Birt. Major was born in 1882 and died in 1929; (For more information about Matilda, see *Book One, Chapter VIII, Section I-III.*)

Section II
Part D-2-5
Purl (Pearlier) Moore and John Keys

Pearlie Moore, daughter of Plas Moore and Lydia Moore, born April 11, 1901 and died November 23, 1994. She married John Keys, son of George W Keyes and Leah Potter Keyes. Pearlie Moore Keys and John Keys had one daughter, Johnann born in 1920 and died September 2009. Johnann married James Ebron. (This could have been the same James Ebron whose father was Franklin Ebron of the Keysville Community of Beaufort County.) James was born January 8, 1913 and died on December 14, 1984. On his Death Certificate, he was listed as being divorced. Johnann Keys Ebron and James Ebron had three children: (1) James T.; (2) Garris and (3) Elnor.

Sometimes after Johnann and James separated, she married Mercer Bullock. Johanna Ebron Bullock and Mercer Bullock had one son, Mercer. According to Johanna's daughter, Elnor, Mercer went to work one day and didn't bother to return home. (According to one of his step sons, Mercer ended up in a nursing home some place in Norfolk, Virginia.)

Section II
Part D-2-6
Tiny Moore and Bessie Moore/Neta Moore

Tiny, son of William P and Sara, was born September 25, 1903 in Blounts Creek and died in Suffolk, Virginia on May 19, 1959. His death was due to an accident involving loading a bulldozer on truck. Tiny married Bessie (Betsey) Moore on November 26, 1924. Bessie was the daughter of Riley and Lydia (Liddie) Jones. (Betsey) Bessie was born April 15, 1903 and died in August 9, 1989. (At the time of Tiny death, he was married to Neta Moore. Tiny and Bessie had four children: (1) Eula Mae, born in 1926. She married Cordies Moore Sr. in Norfolk, Virginia January 24, 1945 and they divorced June 4, 1971. Cordies was the son of William Riley Moore and Isabella Tuten of Bonnerton Community, Beaufort County. Cordies was born March 1, 1925 and died June 13, 2002; (Later, Eula married Luther Scales from Alabama in 1971 in Pasquotank, North Carolina. Luther was born in 1925 and died in 1984); (2) Verna, born on October 4, 1931 and died November 1, 1931; (3) Willie born on September 5, 1932; and (4) Versia Virginia Moore, according to information on her Birth Certificate, (aka Bersia) was born January 2, 1934. Bersia married Henry Champ Burgess on May 14, 1956.

Section II
Part D-2-7
Joshua B Moore and Georgianna Kinsey

Joshua, son of William P and Sara, was born on September 24, 1907 in Blounts Creek and died on September 6, 1970 in Suffolk, Virginia. He married Georgianna Kinsey, daughter of John and Harriet Kinsey, on May 29, 1927. Georgianna was from Cypress Creek, Jones County, North Carolina. In the 1940 U.S. Census, Joshua was living in Richland, Onslow County, North Carolina. Joshua and Georgianna had a son, William born in 1928.

Section III
Part A
Grace Keys and Giles (Gent Giles) Moore

Grace Keys, the daughter of William and Mary Thornton Moore, was born in 1820 and died before 1860. She had children by Gentleman Giles Moore, son of Lucy Moore and John Moore. He was born about 1792 and died before 1860. Grace Keys and Gent Giles Moore had two children: (1) James E. Keys (Keese), born in 1843 and (2) Mary Jane Keys (Keese), born in 1853.

Section III
Part B
Descendants of James E. Keys and Harriett Johnson
(The Original Keys' Town)

James E. Keys, son of Gentleman Giles Moore and Grace Keys was born on February 1843 and died on June 2, 1920. He married Harriett Johnson. Harriett was the daughter of William Johnson and Elizabeth Gaskell. Harriett was on born May 9, 1857 and died on January 9, 1932. James and Harriett were married October 3, 1878. James Keys and Harriett Johnson Keys had five children: (1) George Keys born in 1879. (He never married nor had any children);

(2) James E. Keyes II, born in 1882; (3) Elizabeth Keys, born in 1884; (4) Grace Keys born February 15, 1891and (5) Orlando Keys, born in 1884.

Section III
Part B-2
James E Keyes II and Eva Mitchell

James E. Keyes II, the son of James E and Harriett Johnson Keys, was born in 1882 and died in 1943. He married Eva Mitchell, born in 1887 and died February 22, 1951. Eva Mitchell was the daughter of James Alexander Mitchell and Julia Wiggins Mitchell. James Keys and Eva Mitchell Keys had eight children: (1) Garfield Keyes, born 1909; (2) Alexander M. born 1910 and died November 12, 1976. (Alexander never married nor had any children); (3) Hattie Keyes born 1912; (4) Ruby, born 1915 and died June 27, 1931. (Ruby never married nor had any children); (5) Gertrude born 1921; (6) James E. III born 1919; (7) Hertford born 1924 and died August 21, 1948. (Hertford never married nor had any children and (8) Iola born May 28, 1927 and died June 20, 1927.(Iola never married nor had and children.) Legend has it that James E Keyes II was the father of Lincey C Moore, son of Melisa Moore.

Section III
Part B-2-2
Garfield Keyes and Emma Moore/Mary Stilley Crawford

Garfield Keyes, son of James E Keys II and Eva Mitchell Keys, was born October 18, 1908 and died on October 5, 1972. His first wife was Emma Moore, daughter of Riley and Lydia Moore. Emma was born in 1914 and died before 1941. After she died, Garfield married his second wife, Mary Stilley Crawford. Mary was the daughter of Will and Sara Harper Stilley. Mary was born February 14, 1909 and died February 3, 2002. (Mary's first husband was Henry Crawford born in 1901. There is no other information on Henry.) Mary Stilley

Crawford and Henry Crawford had three children: (1) Rose M (2) Robert and (3) Argie.

Garfield Keyes and Mary Stilley Crawford Keys had six children: (1) George L. born on Jan 12, 1941 and died on March 2, 2001; (2) Ruby born November 28, 1942. (Ruby married Daniel Moore); (3) Edna born Oct 18, 1944 and died March 15, 1993; (4) Dalton born November 27, 1946; (5) Eula born May 7, 1928 and (6) Marian born August 14, 1954 and died in 2009.

Section III

Part B-2-3

Hattie Keyes and James H Foskey

Hattie Keyes, daughter of James E Keys II and Eva Mitchell Keyes, was born in 1912 and died on May 1985. She married James H Foskey, born on April 15, 1909 and died on March 13, 1982. Hattie and James Foskey reared one foster daughter, Mary D Foster, born on June 14, 1937 and died on March 3, 1989. Hattie Keys Foskey and James Foskey had one daughter, Faye. James Foskey was from Aurora, N.C.

Section III

Part B-2-4

Gertrude Keyes and Thelmon Moore

Gertrude Keyes, daughter of James E Keys II and Eva Mitchell Keyes, was on born August 15, 1921 and died on February 14, 2007. She married Thelmon Moore, son of Robert and Sofia Moore. Thelmon was born on October 18, 1921 and died on September 1998. Prior to her marriage to Thelmon, Gertrude had two daughters: (1) Phyllis, (Joseph Moore) and Doris, (father unknown). Gertrude Keyes Moore and Thelmon Moore had five children: (1) Gentry; (2) Arnelia; (3) Donna; (4) Kafer; and (5) Patrick.

Section III
Part B-2-5
James E. Keyes III and Hilda Gaye

James E. Keyes III, son of James E Keys II and Eva Mitchell Keyes, was born in 1919 and died in 2001. He married Hilda Gaye, daughter of Moses and Rosella Pierce Gaye. Hilda was on born May 18, 1928 and died on February 15. 2002. James E III and Hilda Gaye Keyes had three children: (1) James E Jr.; (2) Freddie E., born in 1954 and died in 2017 and (3) Joanus (Bunch).

Section III
Part B-3
Elizabeth Keys and Phillip Keys

Elizabeth Keys, the daughter of James E Keys and Harriett Johnson Keys, was born in 1884 and died in 1946. She married Phillip Keys, son of Joseph and Kezzia Keys. (Note for Phillip: *Phillip was from the William Keyes family, see Chapter 6, Section IV, this document.*) They had three children: (1) Lloyd born in 1908 and died in 1947. (Lloyd never married nor had any children); (2) Keziah born on January 1, 1909 and (3) Joseph born in 1911 and died shortly thereafter.

Section III
Part B-3-2
Kessiah Keys and Joe Johnson

Kessiah Keys, daughter of Elizabeth Keys and Phillip Keys, was born January 1, 1909 and died October 19, 1988. She married Joseph (Joe) Johnson, son of John and Olivia Johnson. Joe was born October 13, 1900 and died March 21, 1976. Kessiah Keys Johnson and Joe Johnson had one daughter; Velma R. Velma, born in 1943 and died May 27, 1999.

Section III
Part B-4
Orlando Keys and Carrie Stilley

Orlando Keys, son of James Keys and Harriett Johnson Keys, was born on April 25, 1885 and died on October 1966. He married Carrie Stilley. Carrie was the daughter of Rumley Stilley and Lula Pritchett Stilley. Carrie was born on June 1890 and died on June 29, 1946. Orlando and Carrie Keys had six children: (1) Booker T. Keys born in 1913; (2) Lula M. Keys was born in 1914; (3) Jessie M. Keys born in 1916; (4) Orlando Jr., born in 1919 and died on August 10, 1934. (Orlando Jr., never married nor had any children); (5) Earlice born on February 17, 1923 and died on April 20, 1923. (The cause of Earlice death was accidental burned) and Earl Lee born in 1922.

Section III
Part B-4-2
Booker T. Keys and Grace Moore

Booker T. Keys, son of Orlando Keys and Carrie Stilley Keys, born in March 31, 1913 and died on April 4, 1993. He married Grace Moore, daughter of William H Moore and Sara Mitchell Moore. Grace was born on February 23, 1913 and died on July 18, 1980. Booker T Keys and Grace Moore Keys had seven children: (1) William O., born on August 24, 1935 and died on August 6, 2006. (William never married nor had any children); (2) Ashley, boron October 15, 1936 and died on April 24, 2001. (Ashley never married nor had any children); (3) Bunyon, born on February 23, 1943; (4) Booker T Jr., born on September 23, 1945; (5) Vincent A., born on December 7, 1946 and died on June 11, 2013; (6) Vance, born on March 20, 1948 and (7) Nancy, born on March 20, 1948 and died on June 30, 2011. (Nancy never married nor had any children)

Section III
Part B-4-3
Lula M. Keys and Golden C Hudgins

Lula M. Keys, daughter of Orlando Keys and Carrie Stilley Keys, born on April 1914 and died on February, 1987. She married Golden C Hudgins, son of John Hudgins and Mary Blount Hudgins. Golden was born on September 16, 1912 and died on March 1987. Lula and Golden died in Chesapeake City, Virginia and were buried in the Keys' Cemetery, Blounts Creek. Lula Keys Hudgins and Golden C Hudgins had one daughter, Thelma, born on November 20, 1936.

Section III
Part B-4-4
Jessie M Keys and John H Smith

Jessie M Keys, daughter of Orlando Keys and Carrie Stilley Keys, born in 1916 and died on March 13, 1993. She married John Henry Smith, the son of Jerry Smith and Mary Johnson Smith. John Henry went by his middle name Henry. Henry was born in 1911 and died on January 3, 1989. Jessie Keys Smith and John Henry had six children: (1) Ledell, (2) Corrine; (3) Jerry C; (4) Mary L; (5) Kenneth and (6) Jean W.

Section III
Part B-4-5
Earl Lee Keys and Benjamin (Ben) Oden

Earl Lee Keys, daughter of Orlando Keys and Carrie Stilley Keys, was born in 1922. Earl Lee married Benjamin F Oden, son of John and Trink Oden. Ben was born in 1921 and died in 2002. Prior to her marriage to Ben, Earl had a son Melvin E Keys, born on September 5, 1940 and died on April 24, 1981. Prior to his marriage to Earl, Benjamin had a daughter, Evelyn M Bell Jordon, born on July 22, 1942 and died on September 1, 2001. Evelyn was born and died in

Washington, N.C. She was buried in the Key's Cemetery, Blounts Creek. Earl Lee Keys Oden and Benjamin Oden had two daughters: (1) Peggy and (2) Beatrice.

Section III
Part B-5
Grace Keys and James Allen Moore

Grace Keys, daughter of James E Keys and Harriett Johnson Keys, was born on February 15, 1891 and died on September 21, 1919. Grace married James Allen Moore, son of James E Moore and Robert Ann Hooker Moore. James Allen was born on August 2, 1896 in Bonnerton, N.C. and died on August 2, 1969 at Cherry Hospital, Goldsboro, Wayne County, N.C. James Allen Moore and Grace Keys Moore had one child, Oswald K Moore. Oswald was born on September 13, 1919 and died on October 16, 2004 at Britthaven Nursing Home of Pamlico, Alliance; Pamlico County, N.C. (Oswald never married nor had any children.)

Section III
Part C
Mary Jane Keys (went by her middle name Jean) and James Milton Moore

Mary Jane Keys, the daughter of Grace Keys and Gentleman Giles Moore, was born in 1820 and died in 1857. She married James M. Moore (went by his middle name Milton). He was born in Blounts Creek in 1835 and died in Blounts Creek. He had at least two brothers: Israel and Benjamin. (According to information contained in Ancestry.Com, Milton and Israel served in the Civil War). Mary Jane Keys Moore and Milton had nine children: (1) William born in 1855; (2) Henry born I 1857; (3) Israel born in 1864; (4) Mary was born in 1866; (5) Bannon born in 1868; (6) Pasty born in 1878. (In the 1900 U.S. Census, at the age of 25, she is living with her brother, William); (7) Milton (Jr) born in 1869, (8) Sara J. born in 1871 and died on November 18, 1917 in Washington, Beaufort County, North Carolina; (She married L E Jones on June 4, 1890) and (9) Emanuel born in 1873.

Section III
Part C-2
William Moore and Roxanna Mitchell

William Moore, son of Milton Moore and Jane Keys Moore was born in 1855. He married Roxanna Mitchell, daughter of James Mitchell and Sivility Mitchell Moore. She was born in 1869 in Blounts Creek and died on 26 Nov, 1949. William and Roxanna Mitchell Moore had three children: (1) Civy I. born in 1887; (2) William H., born in 1889 and (3) Elijah, aka, Big Laj born in 1895.

Section III
Part C-2-3
Civy I Moore and Abner Keys

Civy I Moore, daughter of William Moore and Roxanna Mitchell, born in 1887 and died on September 7, 1930 in Washington Park, Beaufort County. She married Abner Keys, son of Joseph Keys and Kezzia Little. Abner was born in 1892 and died in May 12, 1945. Civy I Moore Keys and Abner Keys had two Children: (1) Anna born in 1914 and (2) Margie born in 1916. After Civy died, Abner married Maggie Jones, daughter of Kit C and Ida Jones, born on May 16, 1910 and died on August 17, 1984. Abner Keys and Maggie Jones Keys had five children: (1) Abner Jr., born in 1936 and died in 1984, (2) Florence M, born in 1942 and died in 2017; (3) Floyd L born in 1939 and died in 2008, (4) Ethel, born in 1934 and died in 1997 and (5) Joyce A. (Mintzy), born on April 22, 1943 and died in 2007.

Section III
Part C-2-4
Annie Keys and Sylvester Washington

Annie Keys, daughter of Abner Keys and Civy Moore Keys, born on December 2, 1912 and died on March 25, 2011. She married Sylvester Washington on August 31, 1951. Sylvester was born in Jacksonville, N.C. and died while living in Blounts Creek on November 22, 2000. Annie and Sylvester Washington had two sons; (1) Alvin and (2) Sylvester JR.

Section III
Part C-2-5
Margie Keys and John Smith

Margie Keys, daughter of Abner Keys and Civy Moore Keys, born on November 7, 1915 and died in Washington, N.C. on December 1999. She married John Smith, son of Henry and Florence Smith. He was born on March 26, 1915 and died on July 15, 1973 in New Bern, N.C. John and Margie Smith reared on child, Della M Smith.

Section III
Part C-3
Elijah Moore and Lina Moore

Elijah (Big Laj) Moore, the son of William Moore and Roxanna Mitchel Moore was born in 1895 and died in 1956. He married Angeline (Lina) Moore, daughter of Alonzo Moore and Fevby Keys. Lina was born in 1899. Big Laj and Lina had seven children: (1) Wort. Born in 1916 and died on January 21, 1967. He was married twice. His first wife was Georgia Little. They did not have any children. (His second wife was Margaret Williams).

(2) William (Knot) born in 1929 and died on September 01, 1070. He never married; however, he had a daughter, Mickey. Mickey mother

was Bettie Little. Bettie was born in 1925. Mickey was raised by Solomon and Clara Moore of the Ware Creek Community;

(3) Lina (Doodle, was born on July 18, 1927 and died o August 22, 1999. She had one child, Glenoria by James Parker;

(4) Hugh (Billy Buck);

(5) Lena (Big Baby) was on born July 18, 1927 and on died August 22, 1999. She never married; however, she had two children by Willie R, son of Betsey A, and Jessie Moore. The children were: (1) Jamie M (Di Di) Moore born in 1958 and (2) Mary L Moore born in 1960;

(6) Paralee was born in 1923 and died June 13, 1954. She had two children: (1) Romanize Winston and Bobby Moore and (7) Mary L.

Section III
Part C-4
Israel Moore and 2nd Laura Wilson

Israel Moore, son of Milton Moore and Jane Keys Moore was born in 1864 and died in 1921. He married 2nd Laura Wilson, daughter of Israel Moore and 1st Laura Wilson. 2nd Laura was born in 1874, and died in 1954 Israel and 2nd Laura Moore had ten children: (1) 3rd Laura, born 1888; (2) Annie, born 1887; (3) Lurancey, born 1890; (4) Lancy, born 1891; (5) James H, born 1896; (6) Niney, born 1899; (7) Climmie, born 1901; (8) Meller R., born 1903; (9) Lillie, born 1910 and (10) Minnie E., born in 1910.

Section III
Part C-4-2
3rd Laura Moore and Nathan Hooker

3rd Laura Moore, daughter of Israel Moore and 2nd Laura Moore, was born in 1888. She married Nathan Hooker (his third wife), son of Nathan Hooker and Matilda Moore Hooker. Nathan was born in 1881 and died in 1937. Laura Moore Hooker and Nathan had three children: (1) Nathan Jr., born in 1927; (2) Calvin C born on February 26, 1929 and died on December 1983 in Hudson, New Jersey; and (3) Christine born on December 29, 1931 and died on June 1987. (Christine never married nor had any children.)

Section III
Part C-4-3
James H Moore and Clara Moore

James H. Moore, son of Israel and Laura Moore, was born in 1896 and died on November 30, 1970. He married Clara Moore, daughter of Bannon Moore and Margaret Blango Moore. Clara was born in 1898 and died on November 5, 1993. James and Clara Moore had two children: (1) Ethel M., and (2) Ulysses. (According to information contained on James Death Certificate, both of his children had deceased.) James and Clara moved to New York and reared a family and moved back to North Carolina. (For more information about Clara, see III, Part F, below.)

Section III
Part C-4-4
Climmie Moore and Dewitt Moore

Climmie Moore, daughter of Israel Moore and Laura Moore, was born on October 12, 1901 and died on August 7, 1992. She married Dewitt Moore, son of Bannon Moore and Margaret Blango Moore. Dewitt was born in 1900 and died before 1925. After Dewitt died,

Climmie married Garfield Thompson, son of C T Thompson and Rosa Thompson. Garfield was born on November 5, 1907 and died on July 1982. Climmie Moore and Garfield Thompson had four children: (1) John, born in 1925; (2) Garfield Jr., born in 1930; (3) Mackler, born in 1933 and (4) Bettie E, born in 1936. (For more information about Climmie, see Section III, Part G, below.)

Section III
Part C-4-5
Minnie C Moore and William David Moore

Minnie C Moore, daughter of Israel Moore and Laura Moore, was born in 1899 and died on June 16, 1966. She married William D Williams (went by his middle name David), son of Hymack and Betsey Williams. David was born in 1879 and died on February 29, 1957. Minnie was David's second wife. Minnie C Moore William and David had five children: (1) Idabel born in 1914; (2) Edgar P., born in 1927. Edgar married a lady from Chocowinity and moved to New York; (3) Cleopatra D., born in 1929. She moved to New York; (4) Julius born in 1932 and (5) Moses A., born in 1933.

Section III
Part D
Bannon Moore and Margaret Blango

Bannon, son of Milton Moore and Jane Keys Moore, was born in 1868 and died on April 13, 1925. He married Margaret Blango, daughter of Lacy Blango and Venus Smallwood Blango. Margaret was born on June 11, 1863 and died on November 5, 1927. She had one brother, Matthew Blango born in 1873. Bannon and Margaret had nine children. They were: (1) Betsy A born in 1894; (2) James born in 1894; (3) Elizabeth (Liza) born in 1894; (4) Clara born in 1898; (5) Dewitt born in 1900; (6) Sara (Little Sara) born in 1902; (7) David born in 1905 and (8) William born in 1911.

(Note: Laci's parents were Harman and Lucretia Blango and their other children were Shade and Gilford).

Section IIII
Part D-2
Betsey A Moore and Jesse Moore

Betsy A. Moore, the daughter of Bannon Moore and Margaret Blango, was born in 1894 and died on February 12, 1977. She married Jesse Blango Moore, (Jesse changed his last name to Moore), the son of Martha A. Blango. Jesse was born about 1891 and died on September 9, 1960. Betsy and Jesse had five children: (1) Geneva, born in 1913; (2) Mahue, (3) Willie R., (4) William E. and (5) Ella Margaret.

Section III
Part D-2-2
Mahue Moore and Edna Roberson

Mahue Moore, son of Jesse Moore and Betsy Moore, born in 1918 in Blounts Creek and died on May 26, 1987 in New Bern, N.C. He married Edna E Roberson, daughter of James and Carrie Roberson. Edna was born in 1921 and died on December 29, 1998 in Washington, Beaufort County. (Prior to his marriage to Edna, Mahue had a daughter, Gaynell, by Clevia Moore, daughter of Edward and Belzorah Moore.) Mahue and Edna had two children: (1) Ivesta and (2) Marvin E.

Section III
Part D-2-3
Willie Moore and Maud Holiday/Mulgray Johnson

Willie Moore, son of Jesse and Betsy Moore, born in 1920 and died December 21, 2009. He married Maud Holiday, daughter of Bryant Stilley and Armethia Hooker. Maud was on born June 23, 1920 and died on November 21, 2001 at Moses H. Cone Hospital, Greensboro, N.C. Willie and Maud had three children: (1) Willie Jr., (2) Dorothy, and (3) Anthony. (*Note: Willie and Maud divorced and later, Willie had two children by Lena Moore.*)

Willie later married Mulgray Johnson, daughter of Johnnie and Lottie Pike Johnson. Mulgray was born in 1926 and died in 1975.

Section III
D-2-4
William E Moore and Ledell Smith

William E Moore, son of Jesse Moore and Betsy Moore, born on March 28, 1932 and died on October 13, 1970 in Fayetteville, N.C. He married Ledell Smith, daughter of John Henry Smith and Jessie Keys. Ledell was born in 1934. (Prior to his marriage to Ledell, William had a son, Bobby, by Paralee Moore, daughter of Elijah and Lina Moore.) William and Ledell had two Children: (1) Campanili and (2) Ronnie

Section III
Part D-2-5
Ella M Moore and Norman Walter Welch

Ella M Moore, daughter of Jesse and Betsey Moore was born on September 22, 1933 in Blounts Creek and died in Bronx, N.Y. on May 7, 2015. She married Norman W. Welch on March 31, 1962. Ella and Norman had six children: (1) Curtis; (2) Walter; (3) Jesse; (4) David; (5) John; (6) Francis.

Section III
Part D-3
James E Moore and Cora L Williams

James E. Moore, son of Bannon Moore and Margaret Blango Moore was born in 1894 and died on April 27, 1935. He married Cora L William daughter of Henry Williams and Jane Williams. Cora was born in 1900 in Washington, N.C. and died on April 28, 1986 in Sinai Hospital, New York City, N.Y. James and Cora had six children: (1) Bannon, (2) McQuinton, (3) Eugene, (4) Annie L., (5) James M., and (6) Archie D., (Kelly).

Sometime after James E died, Cora married Lincey Moore, the widow of Bethany Blango Moore. See Lincey this Chapter, Section II. Part M, below.

Section III
Part D-3-2
Bannon Moore and Idessa Moore

Bannon Moore, son of James E Moore and Cora Williams, born in 1921 and died on December 12, 1976. He married Idessa Moore, daughter of Elijah Moore and Bessie Moore. Idessa was born in 1925 and died on August 11, 1994. Bannon and Idessa had eight children: (1) Dorothy; (2) Bannon Jr. born August 3, 1944 in Blounts Creek and died May 2, 2015Charolette, N.C.; (3) Zachariah; (4) Bessie; (5) Terry D (Pete); (6) Donald D.; (7) Clyde R.; and (8) Samuel. Idessa had a child, Leroy Moore, before she married Bannon. Leroy father's was Jesse Peacock.

Section III
Part D-3-3
McQuinton Moore and Lucy Moore

McQuinton Moore, son of James E Moore and Cora Williams Moore, born on September 16, 1923 and died on April 15, 1990. He married Lucy Moore, daughter of William H Moore and Sadie Mitchell Moore. Lucy was born in 1917 and died on August 28, 2010 in Chocowinity; N.C. Lucy had one child, Eddie prior to marring McQuinton. McQuinton and Lucy had one child, Jessie

Section III
Part D-3-4
Eugene Moore

Eugene Moore, son of James E Moore and Cora Williams Moore, born on July 24, 1925 and died February 8, 1981 in New York. He had one son, Lindsay Ray Moore by Georgia Little. Lindsay was born on July 9, 1942 and died in New York. Eugene and Georgia did not get married. Eugene also had daughter, Gladys Jean, mother unknown.

Section III
Part D-3-5
Anna L Moore

Anna L Moore, daughter of James E Moore and Cora Williams Moore was born in 1926 in Blounts Creek and died in 2017 in New York. She moved to New York at an early age. According to information contained on her Death Certificate, her last name was Brown and she had one son, Sammie L Brown, one daughter, Glory Brown, four grandsons, one granddaughter and twelve great-grandchildren. Anna also had another daughter, Deliver (Sister) Brown.

Section III
Part D-3-6
James M Moore and Rebecca Ham

James M Moore, son of James and Cora Williams Moore was born in 1928 and din May 13, 1960 in Washington, N.C. He married Rebecca Ham, daughter of Lem Ham and Bertha Hamilton Ham. Rebecca was born in 1934 in Aurora, N.C. and died on July 1, 1975 in New Bern, N.C. James and Rebecca had three children: (1) Louise; (2) Velma and (3) Janie M.

Section III
Part D-3-7
Archie D (Kelly) Moore and Coreen Smith

Archie D (Kelly) Moore, son of James E Moore and Cora Williams Moore, was born in 1930 and died in 2017. He married Coreen Smith, daughter of John Henry Smith and Jessie Keys. Coreen was born in 1934. Kelly and Coreen Moore had six children: (1) Elaine, (2) Archie, (3) Eddie, (4) Stevie, (5) Kelvin, and (6) Charlene.

Section III
Part E
Elizabeth (Lizzie) Moore and Josephus Keys

Elizabeth (Lizzie) Moore, daughter of Bannon Moore and Margaret Blango Moore was born in 1897 and died on October 28, 1951. She married Josephus Keys, son of Joseph Keys and Kezzia Little Keys. Josephus was born in 1895. (*Note for Josephus: Josephus was from William Keyes family, see Chapter 7, Section VI, Part A, this document.*)

Section III
Part F
Clara Moore and James E Moore

Clara Moore, daughter of Bannon Moore and Margaret Blango Moore was born in 1898 and died on November 5, 1993. She married James E Moore the son of Israel Moore and Laura Moore. (See Section III, Part C-4-3, above.)

Section III
Part G
Dewitt Moore and Climmie Moore

Dewitt Moore, son of Bannon Moore and Margaret Blango Moore was born in 1900 and died before 1925. He married Climmie Moore, the daughter of Israel Moore and Laura Wilson. (See Section III, Part C-4-4, above.)

Section III
Part H
Sara (Little Sara) Moore and Emanuel Moore

Sara Moore (Little Sara), daughter of Bannon and Margaret Blango Moore was born in 1901 and died on September 2, 1996 in Washington, N.C. She married Emanuel Moore son of Emanuel Moore and Melisa Keys. Emanuel was born in 1905 and died on January 25, 1985 in Washington, N.C. Sara and Emanuel did not have any children.

Section II
Part I
David Moore and Lottie Smith

David Moore, son of Bannon Moore and Margaret Blango Moore was born in 1905 and died on September 22, 1980. He married

Lottie Smith, born on October 10, 1906 and died in Brooklyn, King, New York on April 25, 1983. David Moore and Lottie Smith Moore had three children: (1) Helen E., born in 1926, (2) Kadester born in 1927 and died on May 9, 2010 in Raleigh, N.C. and (3) Cortis L., born in 1928. (After their children were born, David and Lottie moved to New York). (According to her Obituary Kadester was married on December 24, 1955 to Rema Elkin Everett. Kadester and Rema had a daughter, Regina K Everett (Harley) and one granddaughter, Jilaina Chrisma Harley.)

Section III
Part J
William Arthur Moore and Cora J. Peacock

William Arthur Moore, son of Bannon Moore and Margaret Blango Moore, was born on November 4, 1911 and died on June 28, 1986. He married Cora J. Peacock, daughter of Munroe and Gertrude Peacock. She was born in South Creek in 1912. William and Cora did not have any children.

Section III
Part K
Milton (Jr) Moore and Georgiana Moore

Milton (Jr) Moore, son of Milton Moore and Jane Keys Moore was born in 1904. He married Georgiana Moore. She was born in 1877. Milton and Georgiana Moore had two children: (1) Mary J., born in 1895 and (2) Jessie born in 1889.

Section III
Part L
Emanuel Moore and Melissa Keys

Emanuel Moore, son of Milton Moore and Jane Keys Moore was born in 1873 and died on April 30, 1918. He married Melissa Keys, daughter of Israel A. Moore and Fevby Keys. Melissa was born in 1877. Emanuel Moore and Melissa Keys Moore had four children: (1) Lincey C., born in 1901; (Sara (Big Sara) born in 1904; (3) Emanuel born 1905 and (4) Vinettie, born in 1908

Section III
Part L-2
Lincey Moore and Bethany Blango

Lincey Cesar Moore, son of Emanuel Moore and Melisa Keys Moore was born in 1901 and died on February 11, 1968. He Married Bethany Blango, daughter of Martha Blango and Emanuel Moore. Bethany was born in 1902 and died on February 19, 1934. Cesar Moore and Bethany Blango Moore had three children: (1) Roscoe born in 1923; (2) Lincey Jr. born in 1930 and died in 1979 in New York. (Lincey did not marry nor had any children) and (3) William R. (Little Honey). Little Honey was born in 1934 and died on August 12, 1965. (Little Honey never married nor had any children.)

Sometime after Bethany died; Lincey married Cora Williams Moore, widower of James H Moore.

Section III
Part L-3
Roscoe Moore and Elizabeth Moore

Roscoe Moore, son of Lincey Cesar (went by his middle name Cesar) and Bethany Blango. Moore was born on July 5, 1923 and died on April 13, 2002. He married Elizabeth Moore. They had five children: (1) Esther, (2) Roscoe Jr., (3) Daisy, (4) Mary E., and (5) Gloria.

Section III
Part M
Lincey C Moore and Cora Williams Moore

Lincey Cesar Moore, widower of Bethany Blango and the son of Emanuel Moore and Melissa Keys Moore, was born in 1901 and died on February 11, 1968. He married Cora Williams, widower of James E Moore. Cora was born in 1900 and died on April 28, 1986. Cesar and Cora had four children: (1) Cora O., (2) Abraham, (3) Henry, and (4) Samuel.

Section III
Part M-2
Cora O Moore and William W Little

Cora O Moore, the daughter of Lincey C and Cora Williams Moore, was born in 1936. She married William W Little, the son of Cliff and Carrier Little. William was born on January 10, 1932 and died on July 2010 in Lake City Florence, South Carolina. Cora Moore Little and William W had three children: (1) Eddy W; (2) William Ervin and (3) Mona D.

Section III
Part N
Sara (Big Sara) Moore and Filbert Swindell/Thomas (Shake) Little

Sara (Big Sara) Moore, daughter of Emanuel Moore and Melisa Keys Moore, was born in 1904 and died on February 28, 1983 in New York. Big Sara was married twice, the first time to Filbert Swindle. Sara Moore Swindell and Filbert had two children: (1) Theodore, born in 1922 and (2) Gaynell, born in 1925. Her second marriage was to Ralph (Shake) Little, son of Thomas Little and Dolly Pritchett. (Sara and Ralph did not have any children.)

Section III
Part N-2
Theodore Swindell and Lillian Hudgins

Theodore Swindell, son of Filbert and Sara Moore Swindell, born on August 23, 1922 and died on September 1980 in Norfolk City, Virginia. He married Lillian Hudgins, daughter of Louis Hudgins and Osceola Moore Hudgins. Lillian was born on March 29, 1933 and died on July 27, 1997. Theodore Swindell and Lillian Hudgins Swindell had six children: (1) Therosa, (2) Emanuel, (3) Denise, (4) Sabrina, (5) Avery and (6) Theodore Jr.

(Note: John Hudgins' family: His Wife was Mary Blount Hudgins: Children: (1) Louis born in 1910, Wife Osceola Blount Hudgins B. Born on Mar 29 1910 Died on July 27, 1997. Osceola was the Daughter of Abram and Daisy of the Bonnerton Community of Beaufort County. Louis and Osceola had two children: one, Lillian born in 1933 and two, Jessie Mae born in 1926; the rest of John's children were (2) Lillian R, born in 1911; (3) Golden, born in 1913 and (4) Andrew born in 1915; For more information about Osceola's family see Book I, Chapter 6, Section I-VII.;

Section III
Part N-3
Gaynell Swindell and Percy Edward Brown

Gaynell Swindell, daughter of Filbert and Sara Moore Swindell, was born in 1925 and died on January 16, 2000 in Portsmouth City, Virginia. She married Percy Brown, the son of John Samuel and Hannah Ferguson Brown. Percy was born on June 20, 1920 and died on April 24, 2006 in San Bernardino, California. ((About the Brown's family: John Samuel parents were Samuel Wesley and Harriet Fields Brown.) (Gaynell had a son, Johnson Swindell, prior to her marriage to Percy.) Gaynell Swindell Brown and Percy Brown had four children: (1) Percy, born in 1946; (2) Clyde, born in 1948; (3)

Vivian, born in 1950 and (4) Donald, born in 1952. (Gaynell and Percy lived in Virginia. Gaynell and Percy divorced and he later married Lieras G Preciado on June 29, 1961 in San Diego, California. Percy retired from the U.S. Navy.)

Section III
Part O
Emanuel (Little Emanuel) Moore and Sara Moore

Emanuel Moore, son of Emanuel Moore and Melisa Keys Moore was born in 1905 and died in 1985. He married Sara Moore, daughter of Bannon Moore and Margaret Blango. Sara was born in 1901 and died in 1996; (*Note: Although Emanuel is listed as the father of Little Emanuel, Orlando Keys was his father; Little Emanuel acknowledges this information before he died.*)

Section III
Part P
Vinettie Moore and David Minor

Vinettie Moore, the daughter of Emanuel Moore and Melisa Keys Moore, born in 1908 and died on January 30, 1954. She married David Minor, son of George Minor and Martha Lewis Minor. David was born in October 15, 1905 and died June 28, 1961. (I can't find any evidence where Vinettie Moore Minor and David Minor had any children.)

Section IV
Part A
William (Jr.) Keys and Visa Keys

William Jr. Keys, the son of William and Mary Thornton, was born in 1821. In the 1850 U.S. Census, William is living in Blounts Creek, North Carolina in the household of Wineford Blango. In the 1860 U.S. Census, he is married to Visa Keys and they are living in the Swift Creek area of Craven County. They were married by Marriage

Bond on December 29, 1845 with the bond listed as "William Keais" with Stephen Moore being the bondsman. William and Visa had 6 children: (1) William born 1846; (2) Charles, born in 1847; (3) Caroline, born in 1850; (4) Laura, born in 1853; (5) Isaac, born in 1856 and (6) Salix, born in 1858

Section IV

Part B

Charles Keys Sr. and Tamar Bell/Martha Blunt

Charles Sr Keyes, the son of William and Visa Keys, was born on March 26, 1847 at the residence of Father Dairy Bell. In the 1870 U.S Census, Charles is single and working as a farm "labourer" for Eli Cobb in Swift Creek. Charles married Tamar Bell on March 26, 1871. Tamar was born in 1850. Charles and Tamar Bell Keyes had 15 children and they lived in Craven County (Township 1), North Carolina until early 1903. The 1880 U.S. Census has a record of 6 children: (1) Carrie Caroline, born 1871: (2) Charity, born 1872: (3) Ellen (Ella), born 1874; (4) Amandia, born 1876; (5) Francis, born 1879 and (6) Charles Jr., born 1880 The 1900 U.S. Census accounted for the other children as follows: (7) Florence, born in 1882; (8) Mary J, born in 1883 (1886); (9) Augusta, born in 1886; (10) (Anita) Netey, born in 1888; (11) (Lalah) Lola, born in 1890; (12) Sadie, born in 1893; (13) Bertha, born in 1893; (14) Bessie F., born in 1899 and (15) (Mattie) Mathie L, born in 1899. Tamar died sometime before 1915 and Charles married Martha in 1915.

Charles Keys Sr. and Martha Dickerson Blunt – Second Wife

Charles Sr. Keys, the son of William and Visa Keys, was born in 1847. He married Martha Blunt in Pamlico County March 7, 1915 Martha was born in 1865. Listed in Charles and Martha Dickerson Blunt Keys household according to the 1920 U.S. Census were the following children: (1) Madie, born in 1908. (Madie married Mack Howard Moore of Blounts Creek); (2) Jefferson, born in 1910; (3) Marthy, born in 1914; (4) Earnest, born in 1915 and (5) Betty (Rebecca) Blunt, born in 1918. (Since these children were born before Charles and Martha got married, they may have been Martha's by a previous marriage.)

Section IV
Part B-2
Carrie Carolina Keys and John A Dixon

Carrie Carolina Keys, the daughter of Charles and Tamar Bell Keys, was born in 1871. She married John A Dixon. John was born in 1865 and was the son of Allen and Mary J Dixon. Carrie Carolina Keys Dixon and John had four children: (1) Emma J, born in 1894 and died on July 16, 1975; (2) James A, born in 1895; (3) Noah McKinley, born in 1896 and (4) Charles H, born in 1899.

Section IV
Part B-3
Ella/Ellen Keys and David Coward

"Ella Keys, the daughter of Charles and Tamar Bell Keys, was born in 1876 and died October 8, 1934. She married David Coward. David was born in 1873 and died August 22, 1949. His parents were David and Chensie Cherry Coward. Ella Keys Coward and David had seven children: (1) Penina, born in 1899; (2) Clyde, Born in 1903; (3) Cherry, born in 1906; (4) Gilbert born in 1907; (5) Lesley, born in 1912; (6) Farris born in 1916 and (7) Lillian born in 1920.

Section IV
Part B-4
Amandia (Amanda) Keys and Henry J Keys

Amanda Keys, the daughter of Charles and Tamar Bell Keys, was born on May 6, 1876 and died on July 19, 1959. She married Henry J. Keys. Henry was born in 1876 and died in 1976. Amanda and Henry J Keys had 6 children: (1) Carrie born in 1902; (2) Gilbert born in 1905;

(3) Tames born in 1908; (4) Lorena born in 1912; (5) Amand O., in born 1915 and (6) Lela in born 1917.

Section IV
Part B-5
Charles Keys Jr. and Daisy Dudley/Charity King/Chole Lane

Charles Keys Jr., the son of Charles and Tamar Bell Keys, was living in Swift Creek, Craven County in 1880 and died on March 16, 1964 in New Bern, Craven County. He was married three times:

His first wife was Daisy Dudley, born in 1882. They were married on May 4, 1902. Charles and Daisy Dudley Keys had one child, Minnie E, born on March 14, 1903. Minnie married Andrew Lindsey. Andrew was born on May 15, 1900 and died on March 7, 1926. Andrew parents were Wm and Martha Lindsey

His second wife was Charity Grace King of Newport, N.C. They were married on December 23, 1908. Charity was born in 1886 and died in 1926. Charles and Charity Grace King Keys had three children: (1) Lillian born on February 7, 1913 and died on February 25, 1972; (2) Charles III, born on March 4, 1915 and died as a youngster and (3) Franklin, born on August 2, 1920 and died as a youngster.

His third wife was Chole Lane, the daughter of Elijah and Clara Gilliam Lane. Chole was born in 1892 and died on March 25, 1925. Charles and Chole were married on April 20, 1921. They did not have any children.

Section IV
Part B-6
Florence Keyes and J D Aldridge

Florence Keyes, the daughter of Charles and Tamar Bell Keyes, was born in 1882. She married J. D. Aldridge on April 22, 1906. J. D. was the son of Simon and Fannie Aldridge. He was born in 1883.

Section IV
Part B-7
Mary J Keyes

Mary J Keyes, the daughter of Charles and Tamar Keyes, was born in 1883 and died on May 26, 1915 in New Bern, North Carolina. According to information contained in the 1900 U.S. Census, Mary was born in 1883, however, information contained on her Death Certificate indicated the she was born on October 10, 1886 and that she was single. According to family legend, she was referred to as the sister that "took care of her younger sisters".

Section IV
Part B-8
Anita (Netey) Keyes and George A Lindsey

Netey Keyes, the daughter of Charles and Tamar Bell Keyes, was born in 1888 and died on May 31, 1935. She married George Arthur Lindsey, the son of William and Mary Ann Alexander. George was born on January 13, 1891 and died on December 10, 1967.

Section IV
Part B-9
Lola Keyes and J D Wallace

Lola Keyes, the daughter of Charles and Tamar Bell Keyes, was born in 1890 and died on October 4, 1939. She married J. D. Wallace on October 18, 1909. Joseph was the son of Ben and Louisa Wallace. He was born in 1888 and died on February 15, 1965. Lola Keyes and J.D. had five children: (1) Delzora, born in 1911; (2) Dempsey, born in 1914; (3) John, born May 10, 1917 and died on February 2, 2006; (4) Bessie, born in 1921 and (5) Charlie, born in 1924.

Section IV
Part B-9-2
Delzora Wallace and Hullis Jenkins

Delzora Wallace, the daughter of Lola Keyes Wallace and J. D. Wallace, was born in 1911. She married Hullis Jenkins, the son of Green and Alice Jenkins. Hullis was born on February 1, 1904 and died on September 12, 1954. In the 1940 U.S. Census, Delzora Wallace Jenkins and Hullis had one child: Robert Lee, born in 1930.

Section IV
Part B-9-3
Bessie Wallace and Amos Dawson

Bessie Wallace, the daughter of Lola Keyes Wallace and J. D. Wallace, was born on Jun 8, 1920 and die on November 20, 1993. She married Amos Dawson, the son of Joe and Sadie Dawson. Amos was born on April 17, 1917 and died on December 22. 1973. They were married on May 9, 1936. In the 1940 U.S. Census, Bessie and Joe had two children: (1) Marie, born in 1937 and (2) Newaver, born in 1938.

Section IV
Part B-9-4
Charley R Wallace and Ollie L Harris

Charley R Wallace, the son of Lola Keyes Wallace and J.D. Wallace, was born on May 28, 1924 and died on April 11, 2004. He married Ollie Lee Harris December 22, 1951. Ollie was born in 1935. (On Charlie's Death Certificate, he was listed as being divorced.)

Section IV
Part B-9-4
Dempsey Wallace and Clemmie Ethel Nobles

Dempsey Wallace, the son of Lola Keyes and J.D. Wallace, was born on May 10, 1913 and died on Jun 16, 2006. He married Clemmie E Nobles on March 5, 1934. Clemmie was the daughter of Wiley and Allie Nobles. She was born on May 14, 1913 and died on January 14, 2000. According to the 1940 U.S. Census, Dempsey and Clemmie E Nobles Wallace had two children: (1) Jasper, born in 1937 and (2) Dorothy, born in 1939.

Section IV
Part B-10
Sadie Keyes and Joseph A Latham

Sadie Keyes, the daughter of Charles and Tamar Bell Keyes, was born on September 28, 1893 and died on October 23. 1976. She married Joseph A Latham on June 1, 1913. Joseph was born in 1892 and on died March 19, 1935. Joseph was the son of Nathan and Talitha Latham. In the 1930 U.S. Census, Sadie Keyes Latham and Joseph had three children: (1) Vera M, born in 1917; (2) Joseph C, born in 1921 and (3) Mildred, born in 1924. In the 1940 U.S. Census, Sadie is married to Marcellus Bank. (She had another child by Joseph Latham, born in 1936. Sadie must have gotten pregnant prior to Joseph death. As of this publication, Sadie Latham is Sadie L Riggins. Sadie was twin to Bertha; see Section III, Part B-11, below.)

Section IV
Part B-10-2
Vera M Latham and Harvey Tyree

Vera M Latham, the daughter of Sadie Keyes Latham and Joseph A, was born on December 29, 1917 and died on January 10, 1949. She married Harvey Tyree on November 22, 1943. Harvey was born in 1920 and was the son of Mantie and Lommoerson Tyree.

Section IV
Part B-10-3
Joseph C Latham and Hattie Lucille Moore

Joseph C Latham, the son of Sadie Keyes Latham and Joseph A was born in1922 and died on June 15, 1980. He married Hattie l Moore, the daughter of John and Hattie Moore. Hattie was born in 1924.

Section IV
Part B-11
Bertha Keyes and William A Yates

Bertha Keyes, the daughter of Charles and Tamar Bell Keyes, was born on September 28, 1893 and died on November 1, 1950. She married William A Yeats on April 10, 1912. William was born in 1876. He was the son of James H and Carolina Yeats. Bertha Keyes Yates and William had five children: (1) Matthew, born in 1913; (2) Viola, born in 1915; (3) Grace, born in 1918; (4) Ester, born in 1922 and (5) James, born in 1924.

Section IV
Part B-11-2
Matthew H Yates and Mabel Latham

Mathew H Yates, the son of Bertha Keyes Yates and William Yates, was born on August 10, 1912 and died on April 4, 1966. He married Mabel Latham on November 16, 1935; (Mabel was born in 1912 and died sometime before Matthew, on his Death Certificate, he is listed as widowed.)

Section IV
Part B-12
Bessie Keyes and Israel Moore

Bessie Keyes, the daughter of Charles and Tamar Keyes, was born in 1899 and died on February 28, 1958. She married Israel Moore of Bonnerton, Beaufort County on December 5, 1914. Israel was born on October 3, 1890 and died on August 22, 1985. Israel was the son of Elizabeth Ebron and the grandson of Churchill and Barbara Moore of Blounts Creek, North Carolina. Bessie Keyes Moore and Israel had eight children: (1) George Arthur on born June 8, 1915 and died on June 13, 1981; (2) Robert, born in 1918; (3) Annie L, born in October 1918; (4) Charles, born in 1920; (5) James, born May 17, 1933 and died October 7, 1957; (6) Eddie, born July 20 1925 and died April 17, 1999; (7) Elizabeth, born in 1927 and (8) Bessie B, born on September 4, 1928 and died on August 24, 2000. (At the time of her death her name was Bessie B Buck and she was living in Calvert, Maryland.)

Section IV
Part B-12-2
Annie L Moore and Ernest Simmons

Annie L Moore, the daughter of Bessie Keyes Moore and Israel, was born on October 4, 1918 and died on December 19, 1999. She married Ernest Simmons on November 5, 1943. Ernest was the son of Ernest and Alice Summons. He was born in 1906.

Section IV
Part B-12-3
Charles L Moore and Geraldine Moore

Charles L Moore, the son of Bessie Keyes Moore and Israel, was born on March 11, 1920 and died on January 1978. He married Geraldine Moore on July 4, 1952. Geraldine was the daughter of

John and Hattie Moore. She was born on May 17, 1933 and died on October 7, 1957.

Section IV

Part B-12-4

Elizabeth Moore and Robert Jordan

Elizabeth Moore, the daughter of Bessie Keyes Moore and Israel, was born in 1927. She married Robert Jordan on March 26, 1946. Robert was the son of David and Lillie Jordan. He was born on May 11, 1924 and died on May 20, 2003 in Aliquippa, Beaver, Pennsylvania.

Section IV

Part B-12-5

George A Moore and Elizabeth Smith

George A Moore, the son of Bessie Keyes Moore and Israel Moore, was born on June 8, 1915 and died on June 13, 1981. He married Elizabeth Smith. George and Elizabeth Smith Moore had 11 children: (1) Tony A; (2) Andre M; (3) Florine; (4) Deloris; (5) Shirley; (6) Vanessa; (7) Pamela, married Edmond J Moore; (8) Senta; (9) Bernadette; (10) Michael K and (11) James A.

Section IV

Part B-12-5-2

Florine Moore and Jeffery Bragg

Florine Moore, the daughter of George A and Elizabeth Smith Moore, was born on January 29, 1957 and died on November 4, 2013. She married Jeffery Braggs in 2002. Jeffery was from the Aurora Community of Beaufort County, North Carolina. At the time if her death, she had three children: (1) Shemaka; (2) Latonya; (3) Jeffenia; God daughter, Rynika; Step children: (1) Latoshia; (2) Lateffy; and (3) Kasey. (According to information contained on her Death Certificate, she also had fourteen grandchildren.)

Section IV
Part B-13
Mattie L Keyes and William Joseph Moore

Mattie L Keyes, the daughter of Charles and Tamar B Keyes, was born on June 9, 1900 and died on June 14, 1960. She married William Joseph Moore Jr., of Blounts Creek, North Carolina on January 19, 1914. William was the son of Joseph Sr. and Sara Louise Moore (also known Lukie Pender). In the 1930 U.S. Census, they are living in Pamlico County, North Carolina. Mattie Keyes Moore and William J Moore had nine children: (1) William Charles, born on November 9, 1914 and died on May 1, 2003; (2) Sinna born in 1918; (3) Alice born on April 14, 1919 and died on February 24, 2007; (4) Gilbert; (5) Ora born in 1921; (6) Sarah Louise born on June 28, 1922 and died on January 13, 2017; (7) Johnny G, born on April 24, 1925; (8) Jessie, born in 1926 and (9) Ella Marie/Elmarie born on July 3, 1929.

Section V
Part A
Caroline Keys and James H Yates

Caroline Keys, the daughter of William and Visa Keys, was born in 1871. She married James H Yates on April 1, 1881. James was from Aurora, Beaufort County and was born in 1859. James H and Caroline Keys Yeats had three children: (1) John H, born in 1891; (2) Mary E, born in 1890 and died in 1988. (When she died her name was Mary E Smith/Gardner); (3) Sally A, born in 1892 and died in 1967.

Section V
Part A-2
John H Yates and Emma Dixon

John H Yates, the son of James H and Caroline Keys Yates, was born on December 6, 1891 and died on August 27, 1960. He married

Emma Dixon on August 25, 1910. Emma was the daughter of John A and Caroline Dixon. She was born December 1, 1894 and died July 16, 1975. John H and Emma Dixon Yates had eight children; (1) Muriel, born in 1911; (2) Winfred, born in 1913; (3) Lendora, born in 1915; (4) Early M, born in 1919; (5) Lamy, born in 1923; (6) Verna B, born in 1930; (7) Queen E, born in 1933; and (8) Charles R, born in 1935.

Section V

Part A-3

Sally A Yates and Henry Bell

Sally A Yates, the daughter of James H and Caroline Keys Yates, was born in 1892. She married Henry Bell. Henry was the son of Margaretta Bell. He was born June 4, 1880 and died December 13, 1962. Henry and Sally A Yates Bell had six children: (1) Bessie, born in 1907; (2) Tiney, born in 1910; (3) Carrie, born in 1912; (4) Beulah, born in 1916; (5) Vivian, born in 1922 and (6) Addie, born in1927; (In the 1930 U.S. Census, Henry and Sally had a grandson, Jimmie Davis living with them.)

Section V

Part A

Laura Keys and Henry Jones

Laura Keys, the daughter of William and Visa Keys born was born in 1853. She married Henry Jones May 7, 1882 in Beaufort County, North Carolina. Henry was born in 1852. Henry and Laura Keys Jones had three children: (1) Samuel, born in 1890; (2) Laura, born in 1888 and (3) Ada, born in 1885. (In the 1910 U.S. Census, Ada [last name Freedman] is living with her parents and has a child, Martha E Freedman, born in 1907).

Chapter 4
Section I
Part A
Milley Keys

Milley Keys, the daughter Of Milley Keys was born about 1790. In the 1870 U.S. Census she was living In Washington, Beaufort County with her granddaughter. Milley born in 1790 could have been the mother of Milley born in 1805. Milley born in 1805 could have been the mother of Shadrick, born in 1820 and Isiah, born in 1824. Shadrick could have been the father of Milley born in 1850.

Section II
Part A
Isaiah (Isiac) Keys and Rebecca Wiggins

Isaiah Keys, the son of Milley Keys was born in 1824 and died November 12, 1914. He was born in Keysville, Washington, North Carolina. He moved to Long Acre, Beaufort County where he subsequently died. Isiah married Rebecca Wiggins on May 18, 1860 in Craven County, North Carolina. Isaiah and Rebecca Wiggins Keys had two children: (1) William, born in 1868 and (2) Lesline.

Section II
Part B
William Keys and Clarisa Chatman/Mamie Keys

William Keys, the son of Isaiah and Rebecca Wiggins Keys, was born in1868. He married Clarisa Chatman. William and Clarisa Chatman had seven children: (1) Gertrude, born in 1880 (1885); (2) Amay, born in 1884; (3) Amanda, born in 1888; (4) James, borne in 1895; (5) Richard, born in 1896; (6) Oliver, born in 1900 and (7) James, born in

1900. (In the 1910 U.S. Census, his father, Isaiah is living with him. (Oliver and James may have been twins. Clarisa died before 1910 because in the 1910 U.S. Census, William is married to Mamie.)

Section II
Part B-2
Gertrude Keys and Willie Weeks

Gertrude, the daughter of William and Clarisa Chatman Keys, was born in 1880 (1885). She married Willie Weeks, the son of Abram and Annie Weeks. Willie and Gertrude got married on February 27, 1927.

Section II
Part B-3
Richard Keys and Mabelle Ackiss

Richard Keys, the son of William and Clarisa Chatman Keys, was born in 1895. He married Mabelle Ackiss on April 2, 1919. Mabelle was born in 1906. Richard and Mable Ackiss Keys had at least one child, William, born in 1921.

Section II
Part B-4
Oliver Keys and Ada Clark

Oliver Keys, the son of William Keys and Georgia Hines, was born June 1, 1895 and died August 12, 1964. On Oliver's Death Certificate Georgia Hines is listed as his mother. He married Ada Clark on July 30, 1927. Ada was born in 1898. Oliver and Ada Clark Keys had two children: (1) Theodore, born in 1920 and (2) Jane E, born in 1927. In the 1930 U.S. Census, William, Oliver's father, is living with him.

Section III
Part A
Milley Keys

Milley Keys, the daughter of Miley, was born in 1805. She was living in Washington, Beaufort County in 1860. She had six children: (1) Fanny, born in 1843; (2) Benjamin, born in 1845; (3) Miles, born in 1849; (4) Ann, born in 1850; (5) Mary, born in 1852 and (6) David, born in 1850.

Section III
Part B
Miles Keys and Nancy Wilkins

Miles Keys, the son of Milley Keys, was born in 1849 and died April 20, 1920. He married Nancy Wilkins on June 11, 1875. Nancy was born in 1858. Miles and Nancy Wilkins Keys had four children: (1) Frank, born in 1876, (2) Malinda, born in 1879; (3) Oliver, born in 1889 and (4) Estellar, born in 1895; (On Miles Death certificate, Paul Keys is listed as his father). Miles and Nancy lived in the Keysville Community of Washington, Beaufort County.

Section III
Part C
Annice (Annie) (Walker) Keys and Nathan Keys

Annie Keys, the daughter of Milley, was born in 1850 or earlier. She married Nathan Keys (Nathan's last name could have been Keys or he could have assumed Annie's name after they got married). Nathan was born in 1823. Annie had two children; a daughter, (1) Allace (Allice), born in 1864 and a son (2) Willie H, born in 1870. Nathan was Willie's father. (On her Marriage Certificate, Allice's father last name was Walker; however on some of her children's Death Certificates, her last name was Keys.)

Section III
Part C-2
Allace Keys and Allen Payton

Allace Keys, the daughter of Annie Keys, was born in 1863 and died June 20, 1933. She married Allen Payton, the son of Warren Sr. and Susan Payten. Allen was born in Mobile, Alabama on November 27, 1859 and died in Beaufort County January 26, 1912. Allen and Allace Keys Payton had eight children: (1) Flora, born in 1888; (2) Belle, born in 1892; (3) Marjorie (Margia), born in 1893; (4) Annice, born in 1895; (5) Susan, born in 1897; (6) Alice, born in 1900; (7) Edna, born in 1902 and (8) Alliam, born in 1904.

Section III
Part C-3
William H Keys and Sadie (Suddia) Bembry

Willie H Keys, the son of Nathan and Annie Keys, was born in 1870 and died December 24, 1930. He married Sadie Bembry, the daughter of William Bembry and Julia Jones. Sadie was born in 1873 and died January 26. 1917. William H and Sadie Bembry Keys had at least two children: (1) Martha, born in 1895 and (2) David L. born in 1897.

Section IV
Part A
Mary Keys and Augusta Wilkins

Mary Keys, the daughter of Milley Keys, was born in 1852. She married Augusta Wilkins in January 1869. Augusta was the son of Benjamin and Nancy Wilkins and was born in 1845. Augusta and Mary Keys Wilkins had nine children: (1) George, born 1877; (2) Rosella, born in 1878; (3) Samuel, born in 1884; (4) Annie, born in 1885; (5) Henry, born in 1887; (6) James, born in 1890; (7) Ely, born in 1893; (8) Asey, born in 1894 and (9) David, born in 1895.

Chapter 5
Section I
Part A
Mary Keys

Mary Keys, the daughter of Milley, was born about 1789. In the 1820 U.S. Census she is living in Beaufort County with 4 other free colored people. Her children could have been (1) Lacy born in 1812; (2) John born in 1815; (3) Lewis born in 1818 (Lewis' family is so large, it will be listed in Chapter 6) and (4) James, born about 1820.

Section II
Part B
Lacy Keys and Mary Keys

Lacy Keys, the son of Mary Keys, was born in 1812. He married Mary (last name unknown). Mary was born in 1820. Lacy and Mary Keys had five children: (1) Ann, born in 1841; (2) Daniel, born in 1847; (3) Simon, born in 1854; (4) Mary, born in 1847 and (5) Reacey, born in 1844. (Mary and Daniel could have been twins.)

Section II
Part B-2
Daniel Keys and Mary E Moore

Daniel Keys, the son of Lacy and Mary Keys, was born in 1847. He married Mary E Moore on August 23, 1894. Mary was born in 1870. Daniel and Mary E Moore Keys had a son, Daniel S, born in 1899. (Daniel and Mary must have had a daughter who married a Shelton, because in the 1900 U.S. Census, they had a grandson, William A Shelton, also born in 1899 living with them.)

Section II
Part B-2-3
Daniel S Keys and Lillian Keys

Daniel Keys, the son of Daniel and Mary E Moore Keys, was born in 1899 and died December 12, 1941. He married Lillian (last name unknown). Lillian was born in 1900 and died May 26, 1945. Daniel and Lillian Keys had four children: (1) Leonard, born in 1922; (2) Elise, born in 1921; (3) Helen, born in 1926 and (4) James D, born in 1928. (All of Daniel's and Lillian's children were born in New Jersey except James who was born in New York)

Section II
Part C
Simon Keys and Cornelia Morgan

Simon Keys, the son of Lacy and Mary Keys, was born in 1853. He married Cornelia Morgan. Cornelia was the daughter of Charlie and Carrie Morgan. She was born in 1856 in Beat 2, Hinds, Mississippi. Simon and Cornelia Morgan Keys had seven children: (1) Tyner, born in 1889; (2) Georgina, born in 1891; (3) Simon Jr., born in 1893; (4) Cornelia, born in 1895; (5) Estella, born in 1897; (6) Josie, born in 1900; and (7) Carrie, born in 1883. (Simon and Cornelia lived in Mississippi.) In the 1910 U.S. Census, their daughter, Carrie and her Husband, Chesterfield Morgan was living in Simon's household. Chesterfield was born in 1883. Chesterfield and Carrie Keys Morgan had the following children: (1) Minnie L, born in 1905; (2) Analia, born in 1907 and (3) Annstead, born in 1899.)

Section III
Part A
John Keys and Frances Keys

John Keyes (Keese), the son of Mary Keys, was born about 1815. He married Frances (last name unknown). John and Francis lived in

Blounts Creek, Beaufort County and had four sons: (1) John, born in 1843; (2) Zachariah, born in 1845; (3) Southey, born in 1847 and (4) Lewis, born in 1849.

Section III
Part B
Southey Keyes (Keese)

Southey Keyes, son of John and Francis Keyes was born in Blounts Creek, North Carolina in 1847. Southey enlisted in the Civil War Color Troop Military on August 29, 1864 and died while on active duty. He died on December 25, 1865. He was buried in the New Bern National Cemetery, New Bern North Carolina. His mother, Frances filed for his Civil War Pension on April 27, 1888;

Section III
Part C
Zachariah Keyes

Zachariah (Zac) Keyes, son of John and Frances Keyes, was born in 1845. Zac fathered a son, Bannon, born in 1856.

Section III
Part C-2
2nd Bannon (Banner) Keyes and Peggy Moore
(There were two Bannon and Peggy)

Bannon Keyes (Keese), son of Zachariah Keese, was born in 1856. Bannon died in 1946. He married Peggy A. Moore (I could not find out who Peggy's parents were). Bannon and Peggy A. Moore Keyes had four children: (1) William C (Kam)., born in 1888; (2) James Ed, born in 1891; (3) John, born in 1892; (4) Bannon Jr, born in 1894 and died in 1946 and (5) Mamie (Mary) H, born in 1895; Mary father was Israel A Moore.

Section III
Part C-2-2
William C (Kam) Keyes and Carrie Foreman/ Doris Cratch/Willie J Cobb

William C (Kam) Keyes, son of Bannon and Peggy A Moore Keyes, was born in 1888 and died June 14, 1950.

Kam's first wife was (1) Carrie Foreman, the daughter of Willie and Mattie Carter Foreman. Carrie was born in 1899 and died November 11, 1967. Kam and Carrie were married December 2, 1916.

Kam's second wife was (2) Doris L Cratch. Doris was born in 1891, death date unknown.

Kam's third wife was (3) Willie J Cobb. Willie was the daughter of William and Martha Cobb. Willie was born November 19, 1901 and died October 26, 1950. Legend has it, that prior to her marriage to Kam; Willie had a child, born February 14, 1936. The child's name was Willie Keys. On the child's Birth Certificate, Jimmie Keys is listed as the child's father. Jimmie (James) and Kam were brothers. Although in the 1940, U.S. Census, Kam is married to Willie, evidence points to all of the children listed, (13) are Kam's and Carrie's. The Children are: (1) Mattie, born in 1916; (2) Alberta, born in 1919; (3) James born in 1921; (4) William Isiah, born in 1925; (5) Francis Layhu, born in 1927; (6) George G, born in 1928; (7) William A, born in 1931; (8) Carrie L, born in 1935 ; (9) Joseph, born in 1937; (10) Inell, born in 1938; (11) Leona, born in 1938; (12) Parnell, born in 1939 and (13) Rufus, born in 1940.

Section III
Part C-2-2-2
Mattie Keyes and Linwood Martin

Mattie Keys, daughter of Williams C (Kam) and Carrie Foreman Keyes, was born September 3, 1916 and died March 28, 1993. She married Linwood Martin, son of Linwood and Sara Ann Carter Martin. Linwood was born February 15, 1907 and died September 17, 1973. Linwood and Mattie Keyes Martin had eight Children: (1) Linwood (Buddy), born July 9, 1939 and died March 15, 1993; (2) Ernest. Born June 13, 1943; (3) Willie, born December 1, 1946; (4) Queenie; (5) Eddie P, born April 2, 1948; (6) Dorothy M, born March 25, 1951; (7) Debra, born March 11, 1954 and died October 3, 2006, (Debra A Wallace); (8) Dora L. born in 1955 and died April 25, 1956.

Section III
Part C-2-2-5
William Isiah Keyes and Ethel L Godley

William Isiah Keyes, son of William C (Kam) and Carrie Foreman Keyes, was born March 30, 1923 and died October 1975. William Isiah married Ethel L Godley on June 11, 1945. Ethel was the daughter of Joseph and Ethel Godley. She was born June 29, 1925 and died March 7, 2009 in Washington, North Carolina. William and Ethel L Godley Keyes had three children: (1) Oscar, born August 12, 1947 and died June 12, 1998; (2) Willie Inez, born February 28, 1948; (3) CleAuthor, born October 11, 1946 and a step daughter, Ethel, born September 29, 1961.

Section III
Part C-2-2-8
Francis (Layhu) Keyes and Alonza Elijah Moore/SG Gardner

Francis Keyes, daughter of William C (Kam) and Carrie Foreman Keys, was born on July 1927 and died on January 16, 2004. Francis was married twice. Her first husband was Alonza E Jr. Moore, son of Alonza Elijah and Angeline Moore. Alonza was born on May 2, 1933. Francis Moore had 9 children: (1) Alonzo; (2) Francis, born September 9, 1946 and died on April 12, 1969; (3) Nellie (Lissie) married Willie Carter, no children listed; (4) Velma (Tot), born on Mar 24, 1951; (5) Randolph, born on March 24, 1952; (6) Ella Mae; (7) Lynette; (8) JoAnn; and (9) Betty Lou, born on March 3, 1953 and died on December 31, 1953.

Francis second husband was S G Gardner. (On Francis Death Certificate, she is listed as being divorced).

Section III
Part C-2-2-10
Edward Keyes and Vienna Moore

Edward Keyes, the son of William C (Kam) and Carrie Foreman Key s, was born in 1921. He married Vienna Moore on April 28, 1945. Edward and Vienna Moore Keyes had four children: (1) Cora Bell, born on July 16, 1936 and died on May 32, 1991. (When she died, her last name was Weatherington); (2) Lossie, born in 1929; (3) Julia M, born in 1925 and (4) Charlie L, born in 1928.

Section III
Part D
John Keyes and Annie Latham/Emma Tuten

John Keyes, son of Bannon and Peggy Moore Keyes, was born on May 4, 1892 and died on April 11, 1960. John was married twice.

John's first wife was Annie Latham, the daughter of York and Phoebe Latham. Annie was born in 1891. John and Annie Latham Keyes five children: (1) John Y, born in 1913; (2) Gina M, born in 1914; (3) George R, born in 1917; (4) Pensia S, born in 1918 and (5) Annie E, born in 1920.

John's second wife was Emma Moore Tuten of Blounts Creek. Emma was the daughter of Joseph and Katie Moore. She was born in 1907 and died in October 1970. Emma's first husband was Hoyt Tuten. (John and Emma Keyes did not having any children.)

Section III
Part E
David Keyes and Eliza B Keyes

David Keyes, son of Bannon and Peggy A Moore Keyes, was born on March 10, 1900 and died on December 14, 1957. He married Eliza Bowen on April 11, 1918. David and Eliza Bowen Keys had eight children: (1) Lizzie, born 1919 and died 1999. She married Kewby Moore on January 26, 1935; Kewby was born in 1911; (2) Johnnie, born on July 1921 and died on October 12, 1997 in Brooklyn, King, New York. Johnnie served in WWII; (3) Jessie, born on July 10, 1923 and died on December 13, 2002 in Pitt County, North Carolina; (4) Leroy was born on July 27, 1927 and died on December 13, 2002; (5) Christine (Christofer) was born on April 7, 1929 and died on March 19, 1953. Christen married Stephen Floyd on August 20, 1948. Stephen was the son of Ross and Sarah Floyd. Stephen was born in 1926; (6) Arian born in 1928 (7) Sam, born on August 22, 1932 and died on December 3, 2001 and (8) William, born in 1934.

Section IV
Part A
James Keys and Nancy Moore

James Keys, the son of Mary Keys, was born about 1820. He married Nancy Moore on July 26, 1880 and they lived in the Keysville Community of Beaufort County. Nancy was born in 1840. James and Nancy Keys had nine children: (1) William, born in 1851; (2) James, born in 1862; (3) Ivery, born in 1866; (4) Benjamin, born in 1869; (5) Joe, born in 1872; (6) Mary, born in 1873; (7) Ann, born in 1875 and died August 2, 1934; (8) Simon, born in 1877 and (9) Arphilia, born in 1900.

Section IV
Part B
William Keys and Tamar Stilley

William Keys, the son of James and Nancy Moore Keys, was born in 1851 and died in 1951. He married Tamar Stilley, the daughter of March and Harriet Thompson Stilley. Tamar was born on June 7, 1867 and died on April 17, 1927. William and Tamar lived in the Blounts Creek Community of Beaufort County. William and Tamar Stilly Keys had five children: (1) Minnie, born in 1889; (2) Albert, born in 1891; (3) Thurston, born in 1893; (4) Jessie, born in 1895 and (5) Malachi, born in 1897.

Section IV
Part B-2
Minnie Keys and William A Moore

Minnie Keys, daughter of William Keys and Tamar Stilley, was born in 1891 and died on April 25, 1916. She married George A Moore, son of William D and Churchie Moore, on April 15, 1913. William A was born in 1888 and died on July 23, 1954. Minnie Keys Moore and William D Moore had one son, Timothy born on June 9, 1915 and died on Jan 23, 1994. After Minnie died, William A married Clorah Stilley.

Section IV
Part B-3
Thurston Keys and Minnie Moore

Thurston Keys, son of William Keys and Tamar Stilly Keys, was born October 1891 and died August 30, 1964. He married Minnie Moore.

Minnie was born in 1891 and died January 1964. Thurston Keys and Minnie Moore Keys adopted one daughter, Edna L. born in 1930.

Section IV
Part B-4
Malachi Keys and Jessie F Moore

Malachi Keys, son of William Keys and Tamar Stilly Keys, was born in 1899 and died August 12, 1948 in Norfolk, Virginia. He married Jessie F Moore, daughter of William J Moore and Mahala Powell Moore. Jessie was born September 6, 1902 and died December 11, 1959. Malachi Keys and Jessie F Moore Keys had six children: (1) Minnie F born in 1918. (Minnie lived in the Bonnerton Community of Beaufort County ;) (2) Daniel M born in 1919; (3) Cleveland born in 1921; (4) Perinea born in 1924; (5) Almeta born in 1925 and (6) Hazel born in 1928.

Section IV
Part B-4-2
Almeta Keys and David Moore

Almeta Keys, daughter of Malachi Keys and Jessie F Moore Keys, was born on March 20, 1915 and died on September 20, 1982. She married David Moore, son of Renishaw and Doretha Mitchell Moore. David was born in 1918 and died on December 14, 2004.

Section IV
Part B-4-3
Hazel Keys and James A Moore

Hazel Keys, daughter of Malachi Keys and Jessie F Moore Keys, was born September 27, 1927 and died on 17 July, 2006. She married James App Moore, son of James Albert Moore and Lucinda Clark Moore. James was born in 1923 and died on February 19, 1956.

Section IV
Part B-4-4
Rumley Keys and Bedie B

Rumley Stilley, son of Malachi Keys and Jessie F Moore Keys, was born on February 25, 1904 and died in on June 1986. He married Bedie Blackwell. Bedie was born in 1908. Rumley and Bedie had one son: James Alton Keys born in 1926.

Section IV
Part B-4-4-2
James A Keys and Roberta Stilley

James A. Keys, son of Rumley Keys and Bedie Blackwell Keys, was born in 1926. He married Roberta Stilley, daughter of Isaac Stilley and Della Murray. Roberta was born in 1924.

Section IV
Part C
James Keys JR. and Nancy A Moore

James Keys Jr., the son of James and Nancy Moore Keys, was born in 1862. He married Nancy A Moore; (In the 1900 U.S. Census, James and Nancy were living in the household with his parents.) Nancy was born in 1883. James and Nancy A Moore Keys had he following children: (1) Elnora, born in 1900; (2) Mary D, born in 1900 and (3) Joseph B, born in 1905; (Also there is a boy, Frank Moore, born in 1906, listed as old man, James's grandson.) James and Nancy lived in the Keysville Community of Beaufort County.

Section IV
Part D
Benjamin (Ben) Keys and Rhoda Pierce

Ben Keys, the son of James and Nancy Moore Keys, was born in 1869 and died June 22, 1920. He married Rhoda Ann Pierce, the daughter of David and Sara Pierce. Rhoda was born in 1873. Ben and Rhoda Pierce Keys had five children: (1) Sara, born in 1894; (2) Benjamin, born in 1896; (3) Ophelia, born in 1897 and died in 1918; (4) James, born in 1899 and (5) Savannah, born in 1905.

Section IV
Part E
Mary Keys and William B Brown

Mary Keys, the daughter of James and Nancy Moore Keys, was born in 1873. She married William R Brown, born in 1874. William was the son of Mary J Brown (Mary was born in 1852). William and Mary were married May 2, 1900. William R and Mary keys Brown had five children: (1) James W, born in 1901; (2) Joanna e, born in 1904; (3) William R, born in 1905; (4) George W, born in 1907 and (5) Charlie, born in 1909.

Section IV
Part F
Annie Keys and Ephraim William Copeland

Annie Keys, the daughter of James and Nancy Moore Keys, was born in 1875 and died on August 2, 1934. She married Ephraim William on September 28, 1910. Ephraim was born in 1878 and died on March 3, 1913. Ephraim William and Annie Copeland had at least two children: (1) Joseph, born in 1903 and (2) Frank, born in 1904.

Section IV
Part G
Simon Keys and Laura Grist/Sara J Wilkins

Simon Keys, the son of James and Nancy Moore Keys, was born October 24, 1874 and died August 15, 1962. He married Laura Grist, daughter of Lewis Grist and Lucinda Oden. Laura was born in 1875 and died March 21, 1934. Simon and Laura Grist Keys had at least eight children; (1) Dorothy, born in 1895; (2) Danny T, born in 1895; (3) Joseph, born in 1895; (4) Bonnie, born in 1901; (5) Leroy, born in 1904; (6) James, born in 1910; (7) Simon, born in 1912; and (8) Floyd, born in 1915. (Simon married Sara J Wilkins on December 23, 1943. Sara was the daughter of Ben and Susan Wilkins. Her first husband was S.A. Perry the son of M. C. and Amelia Perry. Sara was from Enfield, Halifax County).

Section IV
Part I
Ivry (Ivory) Keys and Margaret Boyed

Ivry Keys, the son of James and Nancy Keys, was born in 1866. He married Margaret Boyed, the daughter of Solomon Boyed and Louisa Boston Boyed. Margaret was born in 1876 in Martin County. Ivery and Margaret Boyed Keys had four children: (1) Benjamin, born in 1894; (2) Walter, born in 1896; (3) Dora J, born in 1902 and (4) Cleophas, born in 1904. Ivry and Margaret lived in Jamesville, Martin County.

Section IV
Part K-3
Frank Copeland and Helen Marie Pierce

Frank Copeland, the son of Ephraim William and Annie Keys Copeland, was born on February 22, 1904 and died on January 27, 1987 in Greenville, Pitt County, North Carolina. He married

Helen Marie Pierce, the daughter of William and Estella Pierce, on September 30 1935 in Craven County, North Carolina. Marie was born in January 17, 1917 and died on July 12, 2002 in Philadelphia, Pennsylvania.

Section V
Part A
(Mamie) Mary S Moore and James H Moore

Mary S Moore, the daughter of Israel A Moore and Peggy Keys, was born in 1895 and died in 1980. She married James H Moore. James was the son of Giles and Margaret Moore. James was born in 1883 and died in 1948. Mary A and James H Moore had three children: (1) Bertha, born in 1910; Mary L, born in 1921 and (3) James H Jr., born in 1925 and died in 1979. James never married; however he had two children: (1) Joyce, mother unknown and (2) Norman Foreman, born in 1948. Norman mother was Rena foreman.

Section V
Part B
Bertha A Moore and Israel Smith

Bertha Moore, the daughter of James H and Mary S Moore, was born in 1910 and died in 2002.
She married Israel Smith, the son of Oliver Smith and Ruth J Moore. Israel was born in 1907 and died 1979. Bertha Smith Moore and Israel had 7 children: (1) Nina; (2) Bertha M; (3) Israel T; James; (5) Deloris W; (6) Laura F and (7) Margaret A.

Section V
Part C
Mary L Moore and Ralph Boskey/Willie Joyner

Mary L Moore, the daughter of Mary S and James H Moore, was born in 1921 and died in 1972.

She married Ralph Boskey, the son of John Boskey and Nancy Moore Boskey. Ralph was born in 1915 and died in 1990.

Mary also married Willie Joyner, the adopted son of Charlie and Millie Joyner. Willie was from Rich Square, Northampton, North Carolina.

Mary L Moore and Ralph Boskey/Willie Joyner dad 12 children: (1) Ralph A Jr. Boskey; (2) Tommy Boskey; (3) Maude Boskey; (4) Deborah Boskey; (5) Goffer Boskey; (6) Maxton Boskey; (7) Eddie Boskey; (8) Ronnie Boskey: (9) Martha Joyner; (10) Jean Joyner; (11) Louise Joyner and (12) Willie Joyner. Mary had another son, Howard Clark."

Chapter 6
Section I Part A Mary Keys
Part A
Mary Keys

Mary Keys, the daughter of Milley, was born about 1789. In the 1820 U.S. Census she is living in Beaufort County with 4 other free colored people. Her children Lacy, John and James are listed in Chapter 5, above. Her son Lewis is listed in Section II, below.

Section II
Part B
Lewis Keyes and Sallie (Sara) A Moore

Lewis Keyes, the son of the Mary Keyes, was born in 1818 in Beaufort County, North Carolina and died about 1875 in Jamesville, Martin County, North Carolina. He married Sara Moore. Sara was born in 1826 and died on December 14, 1932 in Scranton, Hyde County, North Caroline.

(<u>Note for Sara ancestors:</u> 2nd Sara was named after her grandmother, 1st Sara. 1st Sara (Sally), the daughter of John, born about 1740 and 1st Lucy Moore, born about 1779 in Blounts Creek, North Carolina. John and Lucy other children were: (1) Willoughby; (2) Giles (aka Gentleman Giles) my, the Author, 3rd Great grandfather; (3) William; (4) John and (5) Peggy. According to Paul Heinegg, "1st Sara [was] Head of a Beaufort County household of 7 'other free' in 1810 (called Sally Moore) [NC: 118]"

One of these "other free" could have been 2nd Lucy, the mother of 2nd Sara who was born in 1826.

1st Lucy was the daughter of 2nd Rachel and John Punch Moore. 2nd Rachel's mother was Keziah Moore born in 1710. Keziah was the daughter of John and 1st Rachel Shelton Moore. 1st Rachel was born in England perhaps about 1665. For the rest of Sara's family, see Book 1, Chapter 3)

Back to Lewis and Sara

In the 1850 U.S. Census, Lewis and Sara A Moore Keyes were living in Blounts Creek, Beaufort County with two children: (1) Nancy, born in 1847 and (2) William, born in 1849. William died before 1860. In the 1870 U.S. Census, Lewis and Sallie were living in Jamesville, Martin County with the following children: (1) Christopher C, born 1855; (2) Caesar, born in 1857; (3) Charles, born in 1852 (He may have been the husband of Diane Riggs). Diane was born about 1852 in Edgecombe County, North Carolina; (4) Robert, born in 1861; (5) William H, born in 1853 (6) Ivory, born in 1865; (7) Kizziah, born in 1866; (8) Frank J, born in 1869 and (9) Sara Elizabeth, born in 1873.

Section II
Part C
Nancy Keyes and John Taper/Frank Brooks

Nancy Keyes, the daughter of Lewis and Sara Moore Keyes, was born about 1847 and died February 27, 1918. She married John Taper in 1860. John was the son of John Taper. He was born in 1840. Nancy and John Taper had two children: (1) John T, born in 1866 and (2) Isaac, born in 1865. Nancy 2nd husband was Frank Brooks. They were married in 1890. Frank was the son of George Washington Brooks and Elizabeth Bessie Boston. Frank was born in 1860 and died in 1907. There is no evidence that Nancy and Frank had any children.

Section II
Part C-2
John T Taper and Katie H James

John T Taper, the son of Nancy Keyes Taper and John T Taper, was born in 1866 and died January 1, 1919. He married Katie H James in November 1887. Katie was the daughter of William H and Ruth James. Katie was born on January 3, 1871 and died on September 26, 1937. John T and Katie James Taper had seven children: (1) Sophia, born in 1882; (2) Lena, born in 1890; (3) Johnnie, born in 1892, (4) Ada, born in 1894; (5) Clarence, born in 1896; (6) Katie, born in 1899 and died September 26, 1937 and (7) Gladys, born in 1901.

Section II
Part C-2-2
Lena Taper and Solomon Hodge

Lena Taper, the daughter of John T and Nancy Keyes Taper, was born September 1899 and died April 28, 1939. She married Solomon Hodge on November 30, 1905. Solomon was the son of Joseph George and Emma Lynch Hodge. Solomon was born in 1882 and died April 24, 1933. Lena Taper and Solomon had nine children: (1) Elton, born in 1905, (2) Vernice, born in 1910. (3) Horace, born in 1912; (4) Alexander, born in 1917; (5) Elbert, born in 1919; (6) Bradford, born in 1920; (7) Solomon, born in 1922; (8) Kathrine, born in 1924 and (9) Calvin, born in 1927.

Section II
Part C-2-3
Johnnie Taper and Indiana Boston

Johnnie Taper, the son of John T and Nancy Keyes Taper, was born in 1892 and died on January 1, 1919. He married Indiana Boston, the daughter of Gilbert H and Harriett A Boston. Indiana was born on

September 18, 1894 and died on March 1985 in Flushing Queens, New York. (There is no evidence that Johnnie and Indiana had any children.) After Johnnie's death, Indiana married William McLaurin. William was born in 1896 in North Carolina and died in Manhattan, New York. Indiana and William had a son, Franklin, born on May 5, 1930 and died on May 2, 1975.

Section II

Part C-2-4

Ada Taper and Collins/James E Tyner/Warren W Brooks

Ada Taper, the daughter of John T and Nancy Keyes Taper, was born in 1893 and died January 2, 1974 in Goldsboro, Wayne, North Carolina. Ada married a man named Collins, born in Washington County, North Carolina; there is no other information available on their marriage. Ada married Warren Brooks, the son of George W Brooks and Elizabeth Boston; (There is no evidence that they had any children, however, Warren had a son, Willie born in 1893 and died in 1931.) Ada also married James E Tyner, the son of Jesse E Tyner and Julia Scott. They were married on December 15, 1915 in Martin County. Jesse was born February 6, 1889 in Jamesville, North Carolina and died April 2, 1970 in Norfolk, Virginia. (There is no evidence that they had any children.)

Section II

Part C-2-5

Clarence Taper and Mittie Boston

Clarence Taper, the son of John T and Nancy Keyes Taper, was born in January 1896 and died December 8, 1951. He married Mittie Boston, the daughter of William J Boston and Martha Emily ("Dumpsie") Pettiford in Martin County, North Carolina on October 14, 1917. Mittie was born November 29, 1896 in Martin and died January 4, 1974 in Rocky Mount, Edgecombe County, North Carolina. Clarence and Mittie Boston Taper had four children: (1)

Heles M, born in 1924, (2) Luris, born in 1920; (3) Thartix, born in 1932 and (4) Claris, born in 1935.

Section II
Part C-2-6
Gladys Taper and Abraham Pierce

Gladys Taper, the daughter of John T and Nancy Keyes Taper, was born in 1901. She married Abraham Pierce January 5, 1916. Abraham was the son of John and Leannah Pierce. Abraham was born about 1897 and died December 17, 1952 in Plymouth, Washington County, North Carolina. Gladys Taper Pierce and Abraham had three children: (1) Johnathan, born in 1918, (2) William, born in 1920 and (3) Leon, born in 1922.

Section II
Part D
Christopher C Keyes and Sophia Peele/Florence Gaylord

Christopher Keyes, the son of Lewis and Sallie A Moore Keyes, was born in 1855 and died in 1936 in Martin County, North Carolina. He married Sophia Peele. Sophia was born in 1875 and died in 1892. (In some documentation Sophia's last name is Lanier.) Christopher and Sophia Peele/Lanier Keyes had five children: (1) Christopher F, born in 1888 and died in 1919; (2) James Cedon, born in 1884 and died in Boston, Ma., on October 13, 1913 ; (3) Sara (Sadie), born in August, 1890; (4) Mamie, born in April 1897 and (5) Charles H, born in 1882.

After Sophia died, Christopher C Keyes married Florence Gaylord on April 8, 1896. Florence was born in 1867 and died on April 21, 1945. Florence's parents were Nelson Gaylord and Louisa Shepard Gaylord. In the 1920 U.S. Census, Christopher and Florence Gaylord Keyes are living in Jamesville, Martin County with their three children: (1) Lena C, born in 1900; (2) Rosa F, born in 1897 and (3) Rudella, born in 1903.

Over 225 years of Keys 83

Section II
Part D-2
Christopher F Keyes and Elizabeth Pawell

Christopher F Keyes, the son of Christopher and Sophia Peele Keyes, was born on October 8, 1888 and died on March 23, 1919. He married Elizabeth Powell on October 19, 1915; (Christopher F died in 1919 from the Great Swine Flu epidemic about three weeks after the birth of his youngest son, CB.) Elizabeth was the daughter of Preston and Pally Pawell. Christopher F and Elizabeth Pawell Keyes had four children: (1) Mary Marie (went by her middle name, Marie), born in 1912; (2) Christen, born in August 1914; (3) Daisy B, born in 1916.

Daisy married Raymond Morris, the son of Stephen and Coralie on August 30, 1944. Raymond was born in 1908 and died September 26, 2001. Daisy and Raymond had a daughter, Daisy Rae, born February 10, 1949 in Lenoir, North Carolina. Daisy Rae had a son, Marcus Keyes Morris-Griffin, born October 23, 1989 in Fairfax, Virginia and

(4) Christopher Benjamin (CB), born June 23, 1917 and died July 13, 1966. CB was a deaf mute from birth. He attended the North Carolina School for the Deaf. He lived in Richmond, Virginia for a while and later moved to Greenville, North Carolina. After moving back to North Carolina, he married Dorothy Spencer who was also a death mute. CB and Dorothy did not have any children.

Section II
Part D-2-2
Mary Marie Keyes and Jasper (Joseph) Smith

Mary Marie Keyes, the daughter of Christopher F and Elizabeth Pawell Keyes, was born on August 11, 1911 and died in April 1987. She married Jasper Smith on May 4, 1928. Jasper was born in 1910 and died on March 15, 1980. He was the son of Charlie and Myrtle Smith. Jasper and Mary Marie Keyes had five children: (1) Annie, born in 1931; (2) Doris, born in 1933 and died in 2008; (3) Willie, born in 1933; (4) Beatrice, born in 1936 and (5) Joseph Jr. born in 1939 and died in 2002.

Section II
Part D-2-3
Christen (Christine) and Mathew Lewis

Christen Keyes, the daughter of Christopher F and Elizabeth Pawell Keyes, was born on August 24, 1914 and died on July 5, 2000. She was born in Martin County and died in Pitt County. She was reared by her Uncle, Charles and his wife, Alberta in Norfolk, Virginia. Christen married Matthew Lewis on November 25, 1933. Matthew was the son of James L and Annie Temperance Bass Lewis. He was born November 2, 1910 in Hertford County and died February 14, 2009 in Greenville, Pitt County. Matthew and Christine Keyes Lewis had four children: (1) Matthew Henry Jr., born February 10, 1935; (2) James Reginald born December 15, 1939; (3) Edward Earl born January 12, 1941 and (4) Elizabeth Ann, born August 12, 1946 and died October 1, 2009;

Section II
Part E
Charles H Keyes and Alberta Griffin

Charles H Keyes, the son of Christopher and Sophia Peele Keyes, was born November 30, 1882 and died December 5, 1930 in Norfolk, Virginia. He married Alberta Griffin November 12, 1912. (Alberta could have been the daughter of George and Mollie Johnson Griffin.) Alberta was born in 1892. Charles and Alberta didn't have any children; however, they raised their niece, Christen after her father, Christopher F, died. (See Section II, D-2-3 above).

Section II
Part F
Sara (Sadie) Keyes and Job Daniel/Henry Moore

Sadie Keyes, daughter of Christopher and Sophia Peele Keyes, was born September 8, 1884 and died May 6, 1927. She married Jobe Daniel on March 14, 1906. Jobe was the son of Riley and Lucy Daniel. He was born in 1885. Jobe Daniel and Sadie Keyes Daniel had three children: (1) Sophia E, born 1908; (2) James R, born in 1909 and (3) Samuel L, born in 1911. Jobe B Daniel died on July 2, 1911, in Williamston, North Carolina. Sadie married Henry Moore on June 26, 1912. Henry was the son of Granville and Alvana Moore. He was born in 1884. Henry and Sadie Keyes Daniel Moore had seven children: (1) Lillie B, born 1914; (2) Charley, born in 1915; (3) Luther, born in 1917; (4) Ailaca G, born in 1918 and died in 1965; (5) George, born in 1920 and died in 1986; (6) Granville, born in 1922 and died in 1972 and (7) Mary Alvania, born in 1923 and died in 2008.

Section II
Part F-2
Mary Alvania Moore and Thadious K (T.K.) Woolard

Mary A Moore, the daughter of Sadie Keyes Moore and Henry Moore, was born August 10, 1923 and died December 31, 2008. She married Thadious K Woolard on June 30, 1940. T.K. was the son of Wes and Sara E Woolard. Mary A Woolard and T.K. had four children: (1) Wesley (Sonny), born October 10, 1948; (2) Richard, born September 30, 1949; (3) Doris (Cookie) born in 1953 and (4) Douglas, born August 15, 1956.

Section II
Part G
Mamie Keyes and Mack D Woolard

Mamie Keyes, the daughter of Christopher and Sophia Peele Keyes, was born April 1897 and died in 1925. She married Mack D Woolard on May 25, 1910. Mack was the son of King Woolard and Chelsie Woolard. Mack D and Mamie Keyes Woolard had four children: (1) Crystal, born on June 10, 1914 and died on March 13, 1972; (2) Joseph, born in 1916 and died on October 1979 in Washington, D.C. He married Lucy Ellison. Lucy was born on September 13, 1920 and died on September 10, 1995 in North Carolina; (2) Crystal, born on June 10, 1914 and died on March 13, 1972; (3) Dorothy E, born on September 1, 1920 and died on November 20, 2003 and (4) Mack, born on February 27, 1927 and died the same day.

Section II
Part H
Rudella Keyes and William Bruce Boston

Rudella Keyes, the daughter of Christopher Keyes and Florence Gaylord Keyes, was born October 5, 1903 and died October 5, 1937. She married William Boston on May 28, 1928. William was the son of John Pierce and Missouri Boston. William was born November 3, 1898 and died December 22, 1976. William and Rudella Keyes Boston had two children: (1) Fredrick, born in 1934 and (2) Roscoe, born in 1935. (On March 29, 1940, William married Naomie Ellison, the daughter of Henry and Ella Keyes Ellison. Naomie was born August 26, 1917 and died April 20, 1993. Naomie may have had a son before she married William; in the 1940 U.S. Census, there is a boy, William Ellison, listed as William's step-son and was born in 1938. After William died, Naomie must have remarried; on her Death Certificate, her last name was Gorham. Naomie had two sisters, (1) Lucy, born in 1917 and (2) Annie, born in 1924.

Section II
Part I
Lena C Keyes and Andrew Jones

Lena C Keyes, the daughter of Christopher Keyes and Florence Gaylord Keyes, was born in 1900. She married Andrew Jones on December 29, 1920. Andrew was the son of Will and Ninnie Jones. He was born in 1897. Andrew and Lena C Keyes Jones had five children: (1) Mary, born in 1924; (2) Omar, born in 1928; (3) Haywood, born in 1928; (4) Katlapie, born in 1924 and (5) Carlton, born in 1936.

Section II
Part J
Rosa F Keyes and George Hardison

Rosa F Keyes, the daughter of Christopher F Keyes and Florence Gaylord Keyes, was born April 27, 1899 and died August 12, 1965. She married George L Hardison on December 22, 1923. George was the son of Dane Hardison and the grandson of Aldine Hardison; (Dane was born in 1872 and Aldine was born in 1845.) George was born March 18, 1897 and died April 29, 1959. George L and Rosa F Keyes Hardison had three children:

(1) Nathaniel, born in 1924. He married Quennie Elizabeth Woolard. She was the daughter of Joseph and Lucy Ellis Woolard. Quennie was born about 1936;

(2) Majory, born on October 3, 1924. She married Lonnie H Moore on November 9, 1940. Joseph was the son of Joseph and Ann Moore. He was born on October 30, 1919 and died August 12, 1987 and

(3) Mildred, born in 1929. According to family history, she married a man with the last name Hopkins.

Section III
Part A
Sara Elizabeth Keyes and Benjamin Boston

Sara E Keyes, the daughter of Lewis and Sallie A Moore Keyes, was born in January 1873 and died November 4, 1938. She married Benji Boston on December 16, 1891. Benji was the son of David and Hester Boston and was born in 1867. Benji and Sara E Keyes Boston had 11 children: (1) Willis A, born in 1892; (2) Dollie E, born in 1895; (3) Manford A, born in 1899; (4) Benjamin F, born in 1901; (5) David, born in 1903; (6) James E, born in 1904; (7) Irene, born in 1906;(8) Sara E, born in 1906 and died in 1938; (9) Noah F, born in 1910 and died in 1972; (10) Sylvania, born in 1910 and (11) Ophelia, born in 1913 and died in 1980

Section III
Part B
Wills Boston and Essie Boston (Esell Barton)

Willis Boston, the son of Benjamin and Sara E Keyes Boston, was born in 1892 and died March 18, 1960. He married Essie Barton. Essie was born in 1894. On Willis's Death Certificate, he is listed as a widower; therefore Essie must have died before he did. Willis and Essie Barton Boston had seven children: (1) Nathaniel, born in 1914;

(2) James H, born in 1916; (3) Annie G, born in 1917; (4) William, born in 1917; (5) Mary E, born in 1923; (6) Albert, born in 1925 and (7) Minnie J, born in 1921.

Section III
Part B-2
Dollie E Boston and Willie Brooks

Dollie E Boston, daughter of Benjamin and Sara E Keyes Boston, was born in 1895 and died August 28, 1953. Dollie married Willie Brooks, son of Warren W and Ada Taper Brooks. Willie was born February 16, 1893 and died May 2, 1932. Willie and Dollie E Boston Brooks had five children: (1) Jasper, born in 1914 and died April 18, 1930; (2) Bernice, born in 1916 and died in 1920; (3) Allie B, born in 1920; (4) Vinonia, born in 1922 and died in 1994 and (5) Nancy, born in 1914 and died in 1960. (Dollie must have remarried after the death of Ben; information contained on her Death Certificate, indicated that her last name was Clark.)

Section III
Part B-3
Benjamin F Boston and Hattie Wallace

Benjamin F Boston, the son of Benji and Sara E Keyes Boston, was born in 1901. He married Hattie Wallace on November 26, 1920. Hattie was born in 1902 and her parents were Henry and Susan Wallace.

Section III
Part B-4
Manford Boston and Edith Pitman

Manford A Boston, the son of Benjamin and Sara E Keyes Boston, was born in 1899. He married Edith Pitman on December 30, 1919.

Edith was born in 1898. Manford A and Edith Pitman Boston had at least one child Oliva.

Section III
Part B-5
Irene Boston and Nathaniel Bonds

Irene Boston, the daughter of Benjamin and Sara E Keyes Boston, was born in 1906. She married Nathaniel Bonds on April 7, 1923. Nathaniel was born in 1903 and his parents were Henry and Jane Bonds.

Section III
Part B-6
Noah Boston and Virginia Sykes

Noah F Boston, the son of Benjamin and Sara Keyes Boston, was born in 1910 and died in December 1972 in Philadelphia, Pennsylvania. Noah married Virginia Sykes the daughter of Henry and Bessie Sykes. Virginia was born in 1910.

Section III
Part B-7
James E Boston and Mercy D Moore

James E Boston, the son of Benjamin and Sara Keyes Boston, was born in 1904 and died in 1961. He married Mercy D Moore on January 25, 1925. Mercy's parents were James and Mary Moore. Mary was born in 1906.

Section III
Part B-8
Ophelia Boston and Elmond A James

Ophelia Boston, the daughter of Benjamin and Sara E Keyes Boston was born in 1913 and died in 1980 in Brooklyn, Kings, New York. She married Elmond A James on February 20, 1933. Elmond was the son of Ed and Della L James and was born in 1912. In March 1966, Ophelia's last name was Griffin. (There were no children listed for Ophelia).

Section III
Part B-9
Sylvania Boston and Homer H Gee

Sylvania Boston, the daughter of Benjamin and Sara Keyes Boston, was born in 1910 and died in 1930. She married Homer H Gee on May 3, 1924. Homer was the son of Samuel and Cora Gee. Homer was born in 1903.

Section IV
Part A
Ivory V Keyes and Margaret E Boston/Nancy D Barber

Reverend Ivory V Keyes, the son of Lewis and Sallie A Moore Keyes, was born in 1868 and died February 14, 1932. He was married twice. His first wife was Margaret E Boston, daughter of Solomon and Louisa Boston of Jamesville, Martin County, North Carolina. Margaret was born in 1874 and died 1910. Ivory and Margaret were married in 1893. Ivory and Margaret E Boston Keyes had three children: (1) Benjamin Franklin, born in 1894; (2) Walter, born in 1896 and (3) Dora, born in 1899.

Ivory's second wife was Nancy D Barber, the daughter of William and Mary D Barber. Nancy was born November 11, 1893 and died

March 29, 1985. Ivory and Nancy were married on October 24, 1912. Rev Ivory and Nancy D Barber Keyes had nine children: (1) William S, born in 1904 and died in 1989; (2) James (Jiles), born 1905; (3) Wilbert D, born in 1913; (4) James H. born in 1914; (5) Ivory J, born in 1916; (6) Luellen, born in 1918; (7) Mary J, born in 1920; (8) Benjamin Luther, born February 7, 1925 and died August 4, 1992. (9) Roosevelt, born November 5, 1927 and died in April 1982.

Section IV
Part B
Benjamin Franklin Keyes and Beatrice (Bertie) F Smith

Benjamin F Keyes, the son of Ivory and Nancy D Barber Keyes was born August 13, 1893 and died December 14, 1939. He married Beatrice F Smith, the daughter of Jerry and Renia Brooks Smith. Bertie was born in 1897 and died October 30, 1937. Benjamin and Bertie F Smith Keyes had five children: (1) Maggie, born in 1916; (2) Elmer, born in 1918; (3) Solomon, born in 1920; (4) Benjamin, born in 1922 and (5) Christine, born in 1923.

Section IV
Part C
Walter Raleigh Keyes and Minna G Hill

Walter R Keyes, the son of Ivory and Margaret Boston Keyes, was born October 7, 1896 and died June 2, 1985. He married Minnia G Hill, the daughter of Warren and Pattie Powell Hill, in July 1916. Minnia was born May 27, 1901 and died February 9, 2005 in Brooklyn, New York. Walter and Minna G Hill Keyes had five children: (1) Balligh, born in 1922; (2) Odelsie, born in 1924; (3) Goletha, born in 1928; (4) Nina M, born in 1931 and (5) Novealle, born in 1934.

Section IV
Part D
Dora J Keyes and Wilford Staton

Dora J Keyes, the daughter of Ivory and Margaret Boston Keyes, was born March 13, 1899 and died March 8, 1999 at Fort Washington, Prince George, Maryland. She married Wilford Staton on March 9, 1919. Wilford was born in 1898 and died April 21, 1958. His parents were Moses and Florence Harrington Staton. Wilford and Dora J Keyes Staton had eight children: (1) Moses, born in 1921; (2) Annie L, born in 1922; (3) Bradford, born in 1923; (4) John D, born in 1924; (5) Larrengay, born in 1930; (6) Onward, born in 1933; (7) Flora Jean, born in 1935 and (8) Oscar L, born in 1929.

Section IV
Part E
William S Keyes and Estella James

William S Keyes, the son of Ivory and Nancy D Barber Keyes, was born July 30, 1902 and died August 2, 1962 in Plymouth, Washington County. He married Nancy Estelle James on September 3, 1921. Estelle, the daughter of Edward and Della James, was born August 25, 1903 and died January 25, 1985. William and Estella had three children: (1) Milford, born in 1922, (2) Linwood, born in 1926 and (3) William, born in 1929.

Section IV
Part F
James H. Keyes and Hazel M Credle

James H. Keyes, the son of Ivory and Nancy D Barber Keyes, was born November 26, 1914 and died in October 1976. He married Hazel M Credle, the daughter of Thadeus and Annie K Howard Credle. They were married June 1, 1935. Hazel was born July 10, 1915 and died February 12, 2002 in Brooklyn, New York.

Section IV
Part G
Ivory J Keyes and Viola Ward

Ivory J Keyes, the son of Ivory and Nancy D Barber Keyes, was born on February 10, 1918 and died July 13, 1963. He married Viola Ward on May 12, 1953. She was the daughter of Charlie and Margaret Ward. Viola was born August 6 1929 and died February 7, 2006.

Section IV
Part H
Lewellyn Keyes and Addie L James

Lewellyn Keyes, the son of Ivory and Nancy D Barber Keyes, was born in 1920 and died September 12, 1984. He married Addie L James, the daughter of George and Dora James, October 27, 1941. Addie was born February 22, 1922 and died December 13, 2000.

Section V
Part A
Robert Keyes and Harriet Moore

Robert Keyes, the son of Lewis and Sallie A Moore Keyes, was born January 6, 1860 and died August 22, 1933. He married Harriet Moore, daughter of Isaac and Amie Moore, in 1893. Robert and Harriet had eight children: (1) Sadie (Sallie), born in 1893; (2) Courtney, born in 1894; (3) Lovey F, born in 1896, (4) Bessie, born in 1899; (5) Isaac, born in 1900; (6) Lizette, born in 1902 and died in 1932; (7) Pearlie M, born in 1907 and (8) Harriet, born in 1909.

In the 1900 U.S Census, Robert has three grandchildren living in his household. They were: (1) Allica Keyes, (Sadie) born in 1914; (2) Verner Keyes, (Sadie) born in 1916 and (3) Robert C, born in 1919.

In the 1930 U.S. Census, Robert's daughter, Lizette (Lizzie) had married Isiah Hardison, the son of David Rhodas and Donah Hardison. Isiah was born in 1902. Isiah and Lizzie Keyes Hardison had two children: (1) Susie, born in 1922 and (2) Annie, born in 1924. Also in the household in 1930 was his daughter, Pearlie M who had married Manuel Ruffin. Manuel was born in 1904. Manuel and Pearlie M Keyes Ruffin had a son, Robert, born in 1929. Another daughter, Bessie (Keyes) Hill and her two children, Reba, born in 1923 and Seth, born in 1919 were also living with Robert.

Section V
Part A-2
Sadie (Sallie) Keyes and James Ruffin

Sadie (Sallie), the daughter of Robert and Harriet Moore Keyes, was born in 1893 and died September 20, 1931 in Holy Neck, Nansemond, Virginia. She married James Ruffin in Suffolk, Virginia on April 20, 1921. James was born in Bertie County, North Carolina in 1899 and died in Buffalo, Erie, New York in 1984. He was the son of Jim Askew and Ida Ruffin. James and Sadie Keyes Ruffin had at least three children: (1) William, born in 1922; (2) James, born in 1926 and (3) Levy, born in 1929. Sadie's other two children were Alice, born in 1914 and Verner, born in 1916 also lived with them.

Section V
Part B
J F (Frank) Keyes and Mattie Ebron

J F, the son of Lewis and Sallie A Moore Keyes, was born in 1869. He married Mattie Ebron, the daughter of Robb Baston and Brown Baston. Mattie was born in 1876; (Mattie may have had a daughter; Carry Ebron, born in Hamilton, Martin County in 1907).

Section VI
Part C
Kizziah (Kezzia) Keyes

Kizziah, the daughter of Lewis and Sallie A Moore Keyes, was born in 1853 and died before 1920. Legend has it that Keziah had two partners (men): (1) William Boston, (no other information available) and (2) Whitmel (aka Whit Brooks). Whit was born 1849 to Arrinton Arnold Brooks and Penelope Boston. In the 1900 U.S. Census, Kizziah is living with her mother, Mrs. Sallie Moore with the following children listed as Sallie's grandchildren; (These children must have belonged to Kizziah,) (1) Lewis, born in 1885; (2) Hattie, born in 1892; (3) Mollie, born in 1895 and (4) Charlie, born in 1899.

Section VI
Part C-2
Lewis Keyes and Sallie Pierce

Lewis Keyes, the son of Keziah Keyes, was born in 1886 and died August 19, 1963. On his Death Certificate, William Boston is listed as his father. He married Sallie Pierce, the daughter of John and Leanna Pierce. Sallie was born April 24, 1889 and died August 23, 1949. Lewis and Sallie Pierce Keyes had seven children: (1) Mamie, born in 1908; (2) James, born in 1910; (3) Tuirthy, born in 1912; (4) Elijah, born in 1914; (5) Hubert, born in 1917; (6) Austrila, born in 1919 and (7) Howard, born in 1921.

Section VI
Part C-3
Hattie Keyes and Rufus Hodge

Hattie Keyes, the daughter of Keziah Keyes, was born in 1892. She married Rufus Hodge on December 22, 1909. Rufus was born in 1879 and may have been the son of George and Emma Hodge of Lee Mills, Washington, North Carolina. Hattie Keyes Hodge and

Rufus had three children: (1) Pearly, born in 1903; (2) Alfred, born in 1902 and (3) Felton, born in 1902. (Felton and Alfred may have been twins).

Section VI
Part C-4
Mollie Keyes and James Matthew Pierce

Mollie Keyes, the daughter of Kizziah Keyes and Whit Brooks, was born October 10, 1895 and died August 30, 1964. She married James Matthew Pierce, the son of John and Leanna Pierce. James was born in 1892 and died 18 June 1961. James M and Mollie Keyes Pierce seven children; (1) Walter, born in 1914; (2) Edmond, born in 1919; (3) Bessie, born in 1924; (4) Irdell, born in 1925; (5) Alva, born in 1927; (6) John, born in 1928; (7) Hoover, born 1930;

Section VII
Part A
Charles Keyes and Diane Riggs

Charles Keyes, the son of Lewis and Sara Moore Keyes, was born in 1859. He married Diane Riggs. Diane was born about 1852 in Edgecombe County, North Carolina. Charles and Diane had one son, Spier Keyes, born in 1870 and died March 18, 1916. He married Sara Knight, daughter of Elbert Knight. Sara was born about 1880 and died in 1938. They were married November 14, 1900.

Section VIII
Part A
Frank J Keyes and Claudia Lilley

Frank J Keyes, the son of Lewis and Sara Moore Keyes, was born in 1869 and died in 1915. He never married; however, he had a relationship with Claudia Lilley, the daughter of (first name unknown) Woolard and Macey Lilley. Claudia was born in 1879 and died in 1908. Frank and Claudia had a daughter, Gertrude. Gertrude was born in 1898 and died April 11, 1966. She married David Griffin, the son of Warren Griffin and Amanda Woolard, (David was born May 16, 1897 in Washington, North Carolina and died April 1990 in Baltimore, Maryland.

Chapter 7
Section I
Part A
Joseph Keyes and Kezzia Little
(The other Keyes family in Blounts Creek)

Joseph Keyes, son of William Keyes, was born in 1850 in Moons, Newberry, South Carolina and died January 26, 1935 in Blounts Creek, N.C. (Information on his Death Certificate indicates that he was born in Hyde County, N.C. However, information obtained from his grandchildren states that he was born in South Carolina). In the 1870 U.S. Census, he is living in Moons with his father William Keyes.

Joseph Keyes married Kezzia Little, daughter of Rhoden Little and Sara Smallwood. Kezzia was born in Blounts Creek July 22, 1851 and died November 12, 1936. Joseph Keyes and Kezzia Little Keyes had ten children: (1) Mary born 1898; (2) Abner born 1880 (3) Phillip born 1884; (4) Harriet born 1888; (5) Dicey A. born 1890; (6) Josephus born 1889; (7) Graham born 1894; (8) Romey born 1896; (9) Julia born 1899 and (10) Tiny born 1900.

Section II
Part A
Mary Keyes Moore and Parcy Moore

Mary Keyes, daughter of Joseph Keyes and Kezzia Little Keyes, born on December 10, 1898 and died before 1930. She married Parcy Moore, son of Parcy and Lavinia Moore. Parcy was born in 1860 and died March 20, 1932.

Section III
Part A
Abner Keyes and Civy I Moore /Maggie Jones

Abner Keyes, son of Joseph Keyes and Kezzia Little Keyes, born February 28, 1880 and died May 12, 1945. He married Civy I Moore, daughter of William and Roxanna Moore. Civy was born in 1887 and died September 7, 1930. Abner and Civy I Keyes had two Children: (1) Annie born 1914 and (2) Margie born 1915.

After Civy died, Abner married Maggie Jones, daughter of Kit C and Ida Jones. Maggie was born May 16, 1910 and died August 17, 1984. Abner Keyes and Maggie Jones Keyes had five children: (1) Abner Jr., born in 1936 and died in 1984, (2) Florence M, (3) Floyd L born in 1939 and died in 2008, (4) Ethel, born in 1934 and died in 1997and (5) Joyce A. (Mintzy), born April 22, 1943 and died in 2007.

Section III
Part B
Generation 4
Annie Keyes and Sylvester Washington

Annie Keyes, daughter of Abner Keyes and Civy Moore Keyes, born on December 2, 1912 and died March 25, 2011. She married Sylvester Washington on August 31, 1951. Sylvester was born in Jacksonville, N.C. and died while living in Blounts Creek on November 22, 2000. Annie and Sylvester Washington had two sons; (1) Alvin and (2) Sylvester.

Section III
Part C
Margie Keyes and John Smith

Margie Keyes, daughter of Abner Keyes and Civy Moore Keyes, born on November 7, 1915 and died in Washington, North Carolina in December 1999. She married John Smith the son of Henry and Florence Smith. John was born on March 26, 1915 and died July 15, 1973 in New Bern, N.C. John and Margie Smith reared on child, Della M Smith.

Section IV
Philip Keyes/ Elizabeth (Bessie) Keyes/Lizzie Kennedy

Phillip Keyes, son of Joseph Keyes and Kezzia Little Keyes, born July 16, 1884 and died March 5, 1975 in Washington; N.C He married Elizabeth Keyes the daughter of James and Harriet Keyes. Bessie was born in 1884 and died March 29, 1946. Phillip and Elizabeth had three children: (1) Lloyd, (2) Kessiah and (3) Joseph. Joseph died while he was young. (*Note for Bessie: Bessie was from Milley Keys' family.*)

Many years after Bessie died, Phillip married Elizabeth (Lizzie) Kennedy from Pitt County, N.C. she was born June 9, 1891 and died May 14, 1986 in Washington, N.C. Phillip and Lizzie did not have any children.

Section V
Part A
Harriet Keyes and Nelson Pender

Harriett Keyes, daughter of Joseph and Kezzia Little Keyes, was born in 1888. She married Nelson Pender. He was born in 1890. (I could not find and children for Harriett and Nelson.)

Section VI
Part A
Josephus Keyes and Elizabeth Moore

Josephus Keyes, son of Joseph Keyes and Keziah Little Keyes, born February 4, 1889 and died April 1967. He married Elizabeth (Lizzie) Moore, daughter of Bannon and Margaret Moore. Lizzie was born in 1897 and died October 28, 1951. Josephus and Lizzie had three children: (1) Murphy, (2) Virginia and (3) Veva. (*Not for Elizabeth: Elizabeth was from Milley Keys' family.*)

Section VI
Part B
Virginia Keyes and James M Moore

Virginia D. Keyes Moore, daughter of Josephus Keyes and Elizabeth (Lizzie) Moore Keyes, born March 17, 1925 and died March 11, 2010. She married James M. Moore, born in Bonnerton in 1922 and died in the Washington, D.C. on January 19, 2009. Virginia and James Moore had seven sons: (1) James, (2) Edward P., (3) Kenneth, (4) Claude A., (5) William D. was born October 18, 1958 and died March 16, 2017. (There is no evidence that William ever married nor had any children); (6) Clarence E., and (7) Arthur M.

Section VI
Part C
Veva Keyes

Veva Keyes, the daughter of Josephus Keyes and Lizzie Moore Keyes, was born May 13, 1929 and died March 30, 2016. Veva had four children: (1) Carolyn; (2) Peggy; (3) Keith and (4) Cary. (*Note about Veva: She graduate from Erkels College of Mortuary Science in Philadelphia, Penn in June of 1955. Returning to North Carolina, she became the first female African American Mortician in the state of*

North Carolina. After additional research, she is believed to have been the first female Mortician in the state of North Carolina.)

Section VI
Part D
Murphy Keyes and Anna L Peacock

Murphy Keyes, son of Josephus Keyes and Lizzie Keyes, born July 31, 1923 and died May 20, 2013 in Matthew, North Carolina. He married Annie L. Peacock, daughter of Munroe and Gertrude Peacock. Annie was born in South Creek in 1925 and died in 2011. Murphy and Annie Peacock Keyes had two sons: (1) Ruffin R, born July 8, 1944 and (2) Charles M. D., born September 6, 1946.

Section VII
Part A
Graham Keyes and Carrie Sutton

Graham Keyes, son of Joseph Keyes and Kezzia Little Keyes, was born March 4, 1894 and died September 16, 1988. He married Carrier Sutton, born in December 1905 and died in June 1979. (Carrie's mother may have been Luke Sutton who was possibly from Perquimans County, North Carolina) Gram and Carrie had one child, Graham Randolph Keyes (went by his middle name), born on September 20, 1936 and died on September 27, 2008 in Jacksonville, Florida.)

Randolph married Mary E Staton. (Mary may have been the daughter of William M Staton and Christine Wilkins). According to family history (his cousins) Randolph and Mary E Staton Keyes may have had two children. He and Mary divorced and Randolph moved to Jacksonville, Florida. While in Florida, he married Carolyn Walker, the daughter of Milton Walker and Magnolia Jackson. Carolyn was born on September 28, 1937 in Knoxville, Tennessee and died on April 3, 2009 in Atlanta, Georgia. (There is no evidence that Randolph and Carolyn had any children.)

Section VIII
Part A
Romey Keyes Thelma Green

Romey Keyes, son of Joseph Keyes and Kezzia Little Keyes, was born August 11, 1896 and died January 25, 1992. He married Thelma Green; daughter of Cicero and Mary Green from Pamlico County, North Carolina. Thelma was born January 10, 1907 and died October 8, 1998. Romey Keyes and Thelma Green Keyes had three children: (1) Flora L., (2) Gloria K., and (3) Evelyn.

Section IX
Part A
Julia Keyes / Joseph Stilley/John Murray

Julia Keyes, daughter of Joseph Keyes and Kezzia Little Keyes, was born February 9, 1899 and died February 13, 1968. She married Joseph B Stilley, the son of Edward and Lizzie Stilley. Joseph was born in Edward, North Carolina, about 1890 and died in Edward, North Carolina June 14, 1929. They had one daughter, Husir L., born in 1911. After Joseph died, Julia married the Rev. John Murray. Julia and John did not have any children.

Section X
Part A
Tiney and Josephine Minor Keyes.

Tiney Keyes, son of Joseph Keyes and Kezzia Little Keyes, was born August 12, 1900 and died February 11, 1965 in Washington, N.C. He married Josephine Minor. Josephine was the daughter of Umphry Minor and Nancy Stilley. She was born in Edward, North Carolina December 5, 1905 and died in New Bern, N.C., November 28, 1973.

Josephine had one child, Daniel before she married Tiney. Tiney and Josephine had 11 children: (1) Mary, born in 1927; (2) Leon, born in 1929; (3) Oswald, born in 1930;(4) Euli V., born in 1932; (5) Francis M, born in 1933; (6) Selma, born in 1936 (7) Burnic, born in 1946; (8) Lena B, born in 1938; (9) Joshua, born in 1939 and died in 1943; (10) Lee Toney, born in 1941 and died 2015 and (11) James, born in 1944.

Section X
Part B
Leon Keyes and Emily Wright

Leon Keyes, son of Tiny Keyes and Josephine Minor Keyes, was born in 1929 and died in 1960. He married Emily Wright, daughter of Nathan Wright. Emily was born in 1932. Leon Keyes and Emily Wright Keyes had five children: (1) Leon Jr.; (2) Bobby; (3) Phyllis; (4) Alvin and (5) Emily. Sometimes after Leon died, Emily married Jessie Moore, son of Jacob and Matilda Moore. Jessie was born in 1929 and died in 2012.

Jessie Moore and Emily M Wright Keyes

Jessie Moore, the son of Jacob Moore and Matilda Moore, was born in 1929 and died on September 16, 2012. He married Emily M Keyes. Widow of his cousin, Leon Keyes. Leon was the son of Tiney Keyes and Josephine Minor Keyes (Section B, above). Emily was born in 1932. She was the daughter of Nathan Wright. Jessie Moore and Emily Keyes Moore had two children: (1) Jeffery and (2) Patrick.

Section X
Part C
Mary A Keyes and Clifford O Moore

Mary L Keyes, the daughter of Tiney and Josephine Minor Keyes, was born November 25, 1925 and died October 6, 1990. She married Clifford O Moore, the son of William H and Minnie B Moore. Clifford was born July 11, 1915 and died December 30, 1976. Mary and Clifford did not have any children.

Section X
Part D
Oswald Keyes and Eileen/Fanny/Carrie

Oswald Keyes, the son of Tiney and Josephine Minor Keyes, was born on September 28, 1928 and died on July 18, 1997 in Maryland. Oswald was married three times. Oswald and his three wives combined had four children: (1) Oswald Jr.; (2) James; (3) Donna and (4) Don.

Section X
Part E
Eula V Keyes and John Leslie Moore

Eula V. Keyes, the daughter of Tiney and Josephine Minor Keyes, was in born in 1932 and died in 2018. She married John L Moore, the son of William and Nicey Moore. John was born September 17, 1921 and died October 14, 1994. Eula V Keyes Moore and John L had ten children: (1) Shirley; (2) Josephine; (3) Pearlie; (4) William Tiney; (5) Lessie L; (6) Granuel; (7) Calvin; (8) Jasper; (9) Coley and (10) Lorenza.

Section X
Part F
Francis Marie Keyes and Louis Seville

Francis Keyes, the daughter of Tiney and Josephine Minor Keyes, was born 1933 and died in 2016 in Brooklyn, New York. She married Louis Seville. Francis M Keys Seville and Louis had four children: (1) Louis Jr.; (2) Antonia; (3) Benino and (4) Marie.

Section X
Part G
Selma Keyes and Leatha O Gaye

Selma Keyes, the son of Tiney and Josephine Minor Keyes, was born on February 3, 1935 and died on August 11. 2000. He married Leatha Gaye. Leatha was the daughter of Randolph and Rosella Acklin Gaye. She was born September 30, 1944 and died July 7, 2002 in Orange County, North Carolina. Selma and Leatha Keyes had two children: (1) Selma Jr. and (2) Martha.

Section X
Part H
Burnic Keyes and Mary A McCary

Burnic Keyes, the son of Tiney and Josephine Minor Keyes, was born on February 3, 1935 and died on November 8, 2008. He married Mary Alice McCary, the daughter of Ralph and Virginia McCary. Mary was born in New York in 1935 and died on February 20, 2010 in Newport News, Virginia. Burnic and Mary A McCray Keyes had three children: (1) Burnic Jr.; (2) Michael and (3) Regina.

Section X
Part I
Lena B Keyes and Henry Myers

Lena B Keyes, the daughter of Tiney and Josephine Minor Keyes, was born in 1938. She married Henry Myers, the son of Edward Hill and May Myers. Henry was born in 1936 and died on July 8, 2009. Lena B Keyes Myers and Henry had three children: (1) Vivian; (2) Shauna and (3) Henry Jr.

Chapter 8
Section I
Family Tree Charts

This Chapter gives the readers a chance to trace an ancestor back into history through a family Tree Chart. It contains Family Tree Charts for the following people and an Outline Descendants Report for Milley Keys.

(1) Kee born about 1710 through his father, Thomas Jr., Key born in about 1663 through his parents Thomas Sr., Key born about 1630 and his wife Mary born about 1635. Kee was married to Elizabeth Kee.

(2) Milley Keys who was born about 1755, through her perhaps grandfather, Kee, who was born about 1710. Milley's husband was unknown.

(3) William Keyes who was born about 1774, through his mother, Milley Keys, who was born about 1755 and through her grandfather, Kee. William was married to Mary Thornton.

(4) Charles Jr., Keys who was born in 1880 through his father, William Jr., Keys born in 1821 and through his father, William Sr., Keys born in 1774. Charles Jr., had been married three times: I1) Daisy Dudley; (2) Charity King and (3) Chiloe Lane.

(5) Martha Peggy (dropped her first name Martha) Moore, born in 1831; William Plas Moore, born in 1837 and John G Moore, born in 1850 through their mother, Lydia Keyes, born in 1810 and through many ancestors. Peggy was married to James H Moore. William Plas Moore was married to Sara Ann Lindsey.

He also had two children by a lady named Lydia. John G Moore was married to Patience Moore.

(6) James E Keyes, born in 1843 and Mary Jane Keyes, born in 1853 through their mother, Grace Keyes, born in 1820 and through many of their ancestors. James Keyes was married to Harriett Johnson; Mary Jane (dropped her first name Mary) was married to James Milton (dropped his first name James) Moore.

(7) Lewis B keys, born in 1818 through perhaps his mother, Mary Keys, born in 1785 and through her mother, Milley Keys, born in 1755, Lewis was married to Sara Moore, Line #8 below.

(8) Sara Moore, born in 1826 through her mother, Lucy perhaps born in 1810 through her mother, Sara, born perhaps in 1705 and through her mother, Lucy, born in 1758. Sara was married to Lewis Keys, line #7 above.

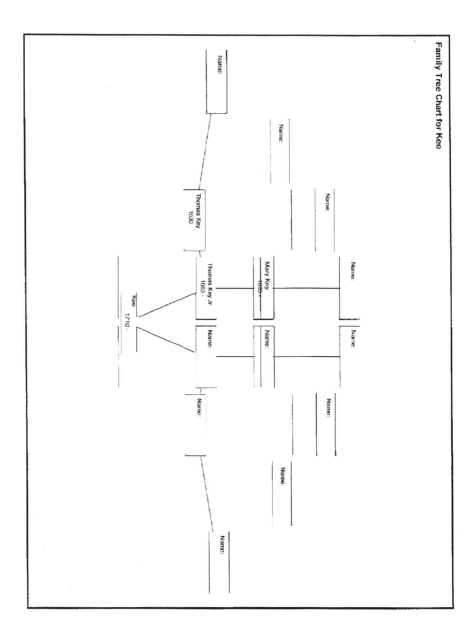

Family Tree Chart for Milley Keys

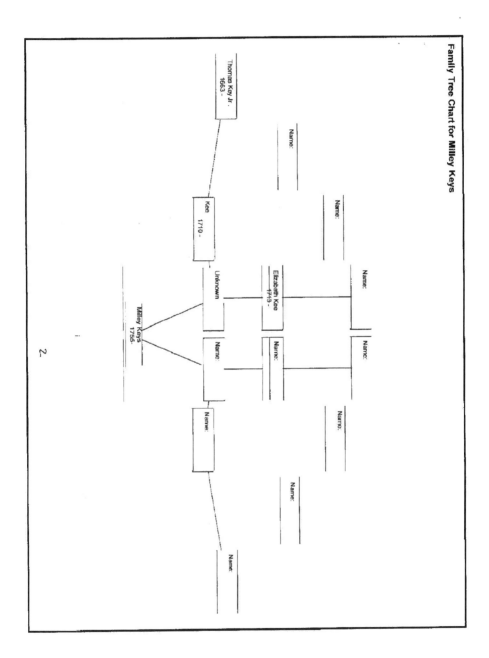

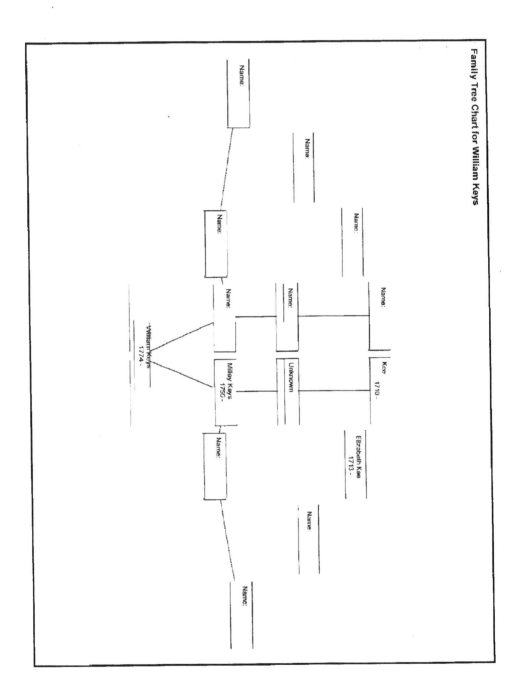

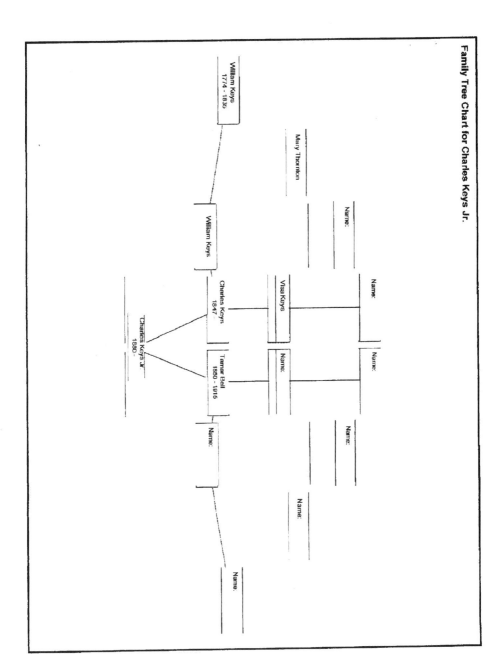

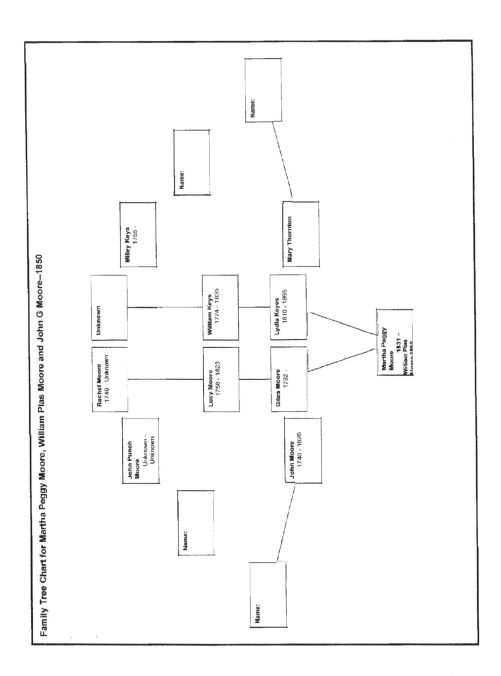

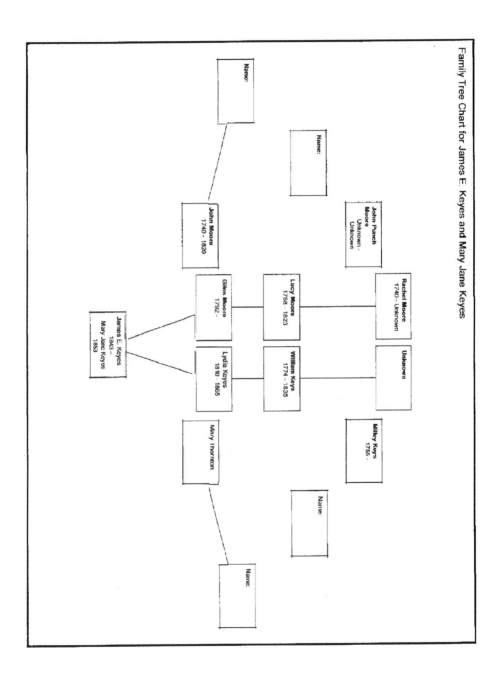

Family Tree Chart for (1) Lewis Keyes Married Sara (Sallie) Moore
(2) Lacy Keys Married Mary (last name Unknown)
(3) John Keys Married Francis last name unknown) and
(4) James Keys Married Nancy Moore

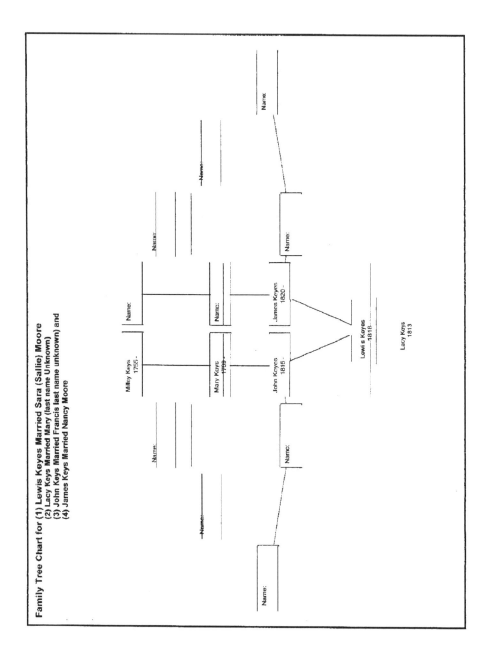

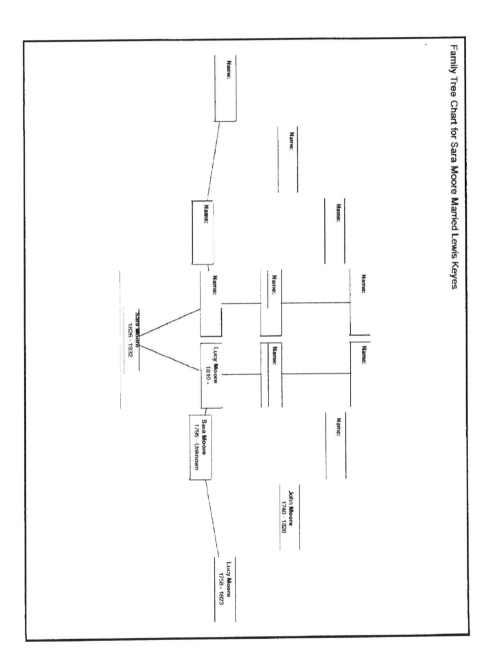

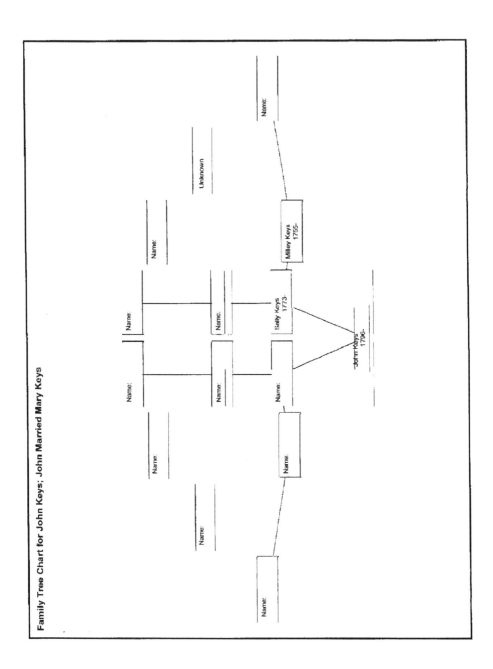

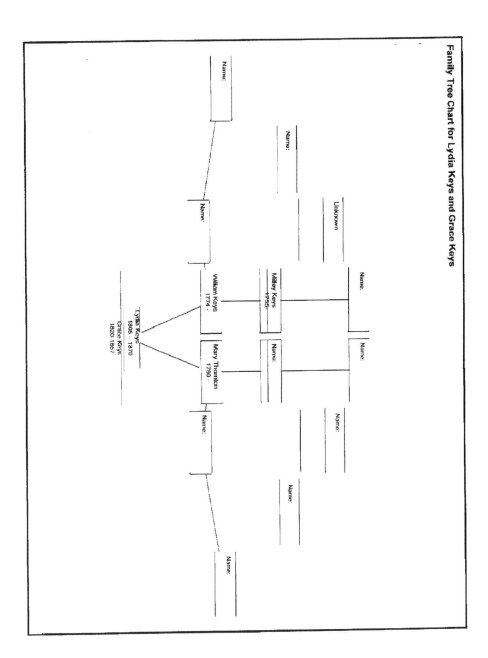

Section II
Outline Descendant Report for Milley Keys

1 Milley Keys b: 1755 in Virginia
+ Unknown
...2 Nancy Keys b: Abt. 1771 in Blounts Creek, North Carolina
+ [unknown spouse]
......3 Southey Keys b: 1805 in Blounts Creek, Beaufort, North Carolina, USA
+ [unknown spouse]
.........4 Southey Keys b: 1823 in Blounts Creek, Beaufort, North Carolina, USA, d: 1881 in Blounts Creek, Beaufort, North Carolina, USA
.........4 Sara Keys b: 1826 in Blounts Creek, North Carolina, d: 1907 in Blounts Creek, North Carolina
+ March Stilley b: 1794 in Blounts Creek, North Carolina, d: 1883 in Blounts Creek, North Carolina
............5 Zachariah Stilley b: 1848 in Beaufort County North Carolina, d: 1923 in Beaufort County North Carolina
............5 Lewis Stilley b: 1850 in Beaufort County North Carolina, d: 1923 in Beaufort County North Carolina
+ [unknown spouse]
...............6 Oliva Stilley b: 1851 in Beaufort County North Carolina, d: 1918 in Beaufort County North Carolina
+ [unknown spouse]
..................7 Frank Stilley b: 1850 in Blounts Creek, North Carolina, d: 1929 in Blounts Creek, North Carolina
..................7 Mary Stilley b: 1866 in Blounts Creek, North Carolina, d: 1914 in Beaufort County North Carolina
............5 Oliva Stilley b: 1851 in Beaufort County North Carolina, d: 1918 in Beaufort County North Carolina

+ [unknown spouse]
............6 Frank Stilley b: 1850 in Blounts Creek, North Carolina, d: 1929 in Blounts Creek, North Carolina
............6 Mary Stilley b: 1866 in Blounts Creek, North Carolina, d: 1914 in Beaufort County North Carolina
......3 Southey Keys b: Abt. 1805 in Blounts Creek, North Carolina
+ [unknown spouse]
.........4 Mary Keys b: Abt. 1804 in Blounts Creek, North Carolina
.........4 Southey (Jr.) Keys b: Abt. 1822 in Blounts Creek, North Carolina, d: 1881 in Blounts Creek, North Carolina
+ [unknown spouse]
............5 Sara Keys b: 1826 in Blounts Creek, North Carolina, d: 1907 in Blounts Creek, North Carolina
+ March Stilley b: 1794 in Blounts Creek, North Carolina, d: 1883 in Blounts Creek, North Carolina
...............6 Zachariah Stilley b: 1848 in Beaufort County North Carolina, d: 1923 in Beaufort County North Carolina
...............6 Lewis Stilley b: 1850 in Beaufort County North Carolina, d: 1923 in Beaufort County North Carolina
+ [unknown spouse]
..................7 Oliva Stilley b: 1851 in Beaufort County North Carolina, d: 1918 in Beaufort County North Carolina
+ [unknown spouse]
....................8 Frank Stilley b: 1850 in Blounts Creek, North Carolina, d: 1929 in Blounts Creek, North Carolina
....................8 Mary Stilley b: 1866 in Blounts Creek, North Carolina, d: 1914 in Beaufort County North Carolina
...............6 Oliva Stilley b: 1851 in Beaufort County North Carolina, d: 1918 in Beaufort County North Carolina
+ [unknown spouse]
..................7 Frank Stilley b: 1850 in Blounts Creek, North Carolina, d: 1929 in Blounts Creek, North Carolina
..................7 Mary Stilley b: 1866 in Blounts Creek, North Carolina, d: 1914 in Beaufort County North Carolina

...2 Sally Keys b: Abt. 1773 in Blounts Creek, North Carolina
+ [unknown spouse]
......3 John Keys b: 1796 in Blounts Creek, North Carolina
...2 Willam Keys b: Abt. 1774 in Blounts Creek, North Carolina, d: 1835 in Craven County North Carolina
+ Mary Thornton m: 03 Dec 1825 in Craven County, North Carolina
......3 Lydia Keyes b: 1810 in New Bern, Craven, North Carolina, USA, d: 1865 in Blounts Creek, North Carloina
+ Giles Moore b: 1792 in Blounts Creek, North Carloina, m: Blounts Creek, North Carolina, d: Blounts Creek, North Carloina
.........4 Martha Peggy Moore b: 1831 in Blounts Creek, North Carolina, d: Blounts Creek, North Carolina
+ James H Moore b: 1826, m: Blounts Creek, North Carolina, d: 1867 in Blounts Creek, North Carolina
............5 Sidney Moore (unk rel) b: 1848 in Blounts Creek, North Carolina
............5 Lydia Moore (unk rel) b: 1851 in Blounts Creek, North Carolina
............5 Edward Moore b: 1854 in Blounts Creek, North Carolina
............5 Riley Moore b: 1856 in Blounts Creek, North Carolina, d: New Bern
............5 William Moore b: 1859 in Blounts Creek, North Carolina, d: New Bern
............5 Isreal Albert Moore b: 1862 in Blounts Creek, N.C, d: Blounts Creek, N.C
+ Fevby A Keyes b: 1863 in Blounts Creek, N.C, d: Blounts Creek, N.C
...............6 Mamie Keyes b: 1891 in Blounts Creek, N.C, d: 16 Nov 1954 in Blounts Creek, N.C
+ Mack Blango b: 1885 in Blounts Creek, N.C, d: Blounts Creek, N.C
..................7 Mary Blango b: 1912 in Blounts Creek, N.C, d: Blounts Creek, N.C

................7 Jessie L Blango b: 1915 in Blounts Creek, N.C, d: Blounts Creek, N.C
................7 John A Blango b: 1918 in Blounts Creek, N.C, d: Blounts Creek, N.C
................7 Mack S Blango b: 1921 in Blounts Creek, N.C, d: Blounts Creek, N.C
................7 Perlie Blango b: 1923 in Blounts Creek, N.C, d: Blounts Creek, N.C
................7 Leonard Blango b: 1925 in Blounts Creek, N.C, d: Blounts Creek, N.C
................7 Edward Blango b: 1927 in Blounts Creek, N.C, d: Blounts Creek, N.C
................7 Asford M Blango b: 1929
............6 Sallie Keyes
............6 Mary S Keyes b: Blounts Creek, N.C
+ James H Moore b: Blounts Creek, N.C
................7 Bertha Moore b: 1910 in Blounts Creek, N.C, d: Blounts Creek, N.C
+ Isreal Smith b: 1907 in Blounts Creek, N.C, d: Blounts Creek, N.C
....................8 Nina Smith b: 1930 in Blounts Creek, N.C
....................8 James E Smith b: 1943 in Blounts Creek, N.C, d: Blounts Creek, N.C
....................8 Bertha Smith b: Blounts Creek, N.C, d: Blounts Creek, N.C
....................8 Isreal Jr Smith b: Blounts Creek, N.C
....................8 Willo Smith b: Blounts Creek, N.C
....................8 Laura F Smith b: Blounts Creek, N.C
....................8 Maraget A Smith
+ Civia Moore b: 1870 in Blounts Creek, N.C, d: Blounts Creek, N.C
............6 Emmaline Moore b: 1896 in Blounts Creek, N.C, d: Blounts Creek, N.C
............6 James A Moore b: 1898 in Blounts Creek, N.C, d: Blounts Creek, N.C

+ Lucinda Clark b: Blounts Creek, N.C, d: Blounts Creek, N.C

...........6 Hugh Moore b: 1899 in Blounts Creek, N.C, d: Blounts Creek, N.C

...........6 Elizabeth Moore b: 1900 in Blounts Creek, N.C, d: Blounts Creek, N.C

+ Kelly Moore b: 1897 in Blounts Creek, N.C, d: Blounts Creek, N.C

..............7 Agnes Moore b: 1917 in Blounts Creek, N.C, d: Blounts Creek, N.C

..............7 Armie Moore b: 1920 in Blounts Creek, N.C, d: Blounts Creek, N.C

..............7 Emaline Moore b: 1922 in Blounts Creek, N.C, d: Blounts Creek, N.C

..............7 Leonard Moore b: 1923 in Blounts Creek, N.C, d: Blounts Creek, N.C

..............7 Roberta Moore b: 1925 in Blounts Creek, N.C, d: Blounts Creek, N.C

..............7 Hersille Moore b: 1927 in Blounts Creek, N.C, d: Blounts Creek, N.C

..............7 Kelly Jr Moore b: 1929 in Blounts Creek, N.C, d: Blounts Creek, N.C

..............7 Ola M Moore b: Blounts Creek, N.C, d: Blounts Creek, N.C

+ Joseph Moore b: 1917 in Blounts Creek, N.C

...........6 Lyddia Moore b: 1901 in Blounts Creek, N.C, d: Blounts Creek, N.C

...........6 Mezowal Moore b: 1903 in Blounts Creek, N.C, d: Blounts Creek, N.C

...........6 Roxanna Moore b: 1905 in Blounts Creek, N.C, d: Blounts Creek, N.C

...........6 Civia A Moore b: 1907 in Blounts Creek, N.C, d: Blounts Creek, N.C

...........6 Edward Moore b: 1909 in Blounts Creek, N.C, d: Blounts Creek, N.C

............5 Maraget Moore b: 1865 in Blounts Creek, N.C, d: Blounts Creek, N.C

+ Giles Moore b: 1856 in Blounts Creek, N.C, m: 15 May 1884 in Blounts Creek, North Carolina, d: Blounts Creek, N.C

...............6 James H Moore b: 1902 in Blounts Creek, N.C, d: Blounts Creek, N.C

...............6 Maggie Moore b: 1908 in Blounts Creek, N.C, d: Blounts Creek, N.C

...............6 Peggie Moore b: 1911 in Blounts Creek, N.C, d: Blounts Creek, N.C

...............6 Lucy Moore b: 1913 in Blounts Creek, N.C, d: Blounts Creek, N.C

...............6 Liddia Moore b: 1915 in Blounts Creek, N.C, d: Blounts Creek, N.C

...............6 Edward Moore b: 1917 in Blounts Creek, N.C, d: Blounts Creek, N.C

...............6 Nicie Moore b: 1918 in Blounts Creek, N.C, d: Blounts Creek, N.C

...............6 Giles Moore b: 1919 in Blounts Creek, N.C, d: Blounts Creek, N.C

.........4 William Moore b: 1835 in Blounts Creek, North Carloina, d: Blounts Creek, North Carloina

.........4 Mary Moore b: 1836 in Blounts Creek, North Carloina, d: Blounts Creek, North Carloina

.........4 Henry Greene b: 1841 in Blounts Creek, North Carloina, d: Washington. N.C

.........4 James E. Keyes b: Feb 1843 in Blounts Creek, North Carolina, d: Blounts Creek, North Carolina

+ Harriett Johnson b: 09 May 1857 in Blounts Creek, North Carolina, m: 03 Oct 1878 in Blounts Creek, North Carolina, d: 09 Jan 1932 in Blounts Creek, North Carloina

............5 Grace Keyes b: 1820 in Craven County, North Carolina, d: 1855 in Blounts Creek, North Carolina

+ [unknown spouse]

...............6 James E Keys b: 1843

............6 Mary Jane Keys b: 1853 in Blounts Creek, North Carolina, d: 1919 in Blounts Creek, North Carolina
+ James Milton Moore b: 1835 in Blounts Creek, North Carolina, d: Bef. 1890 in Blounts Creek, North Carolina
...........5 George Keyes b: 1879 in Blounts Creek, North Carolina, d: Blounts Creek, North Carolina
+ None
............6 None
...........5 James E Keyes II b: 1882 in Blounts Creek, North Carolina, d: 11 Mar 1943 in Blounts Creek, North Carloina
+ Eva Mitchell b: 1878 in Blounts Creek, North Carloina, m: 12 Jun 1907 in Blounts Creek, North Carolina, d: 22 Feb 1951 in Blounts Creek, North Carloina
............6 Garfield Keyes b: 1909 in Blounts Creek, North Carloina, d: 15 Oct 1971 in Blounts Creek, North Carloina
+ Mary E Crawford b: Edward, N.C, d: Greensboro, N.C.
.................7 George L Keyes b: 12 Jan 1941 in Blounts Creek, N.C, d: Washington. N.C
.................7 Ruby Keyes b: 28 Nov 1942 in Blounts Creek, N.C
.................7 Edna Keyes b: 18 Oct 1944 in Blounts Creek, N.C, d: Raleigh, N.C
.................7 Dalton Keyes b: 27 Nov 1946 in Blounts Creek, N.C
.................7 Eula Keyes b: 07 May 1948 in Blounts Creek, N.C
.................7 Marian Keyes b: 14 Aug 1953 in Blounts Creek, N.C
............6 Alexander M Keyes b: 1910 in Blounts Creek, North Carloina, d: 12 Nov 1976 in Blounts Creek, North Carloina

............6 Hattie Keyes b: 1912 in Blounts Creek, North Carloina, d: 28 Apr 1985 in Blounts Creek, North Carloina
+ James Foskey b: Aurora, North Carolina, d: Blounts Creek, N.C
............6 Rubie Keyes b: 1915 in Blounts Creek, North Carloina, d: 27 Jun 1931 in Blounts Creek, North Carloina
............6 James E Keyes III b: 1919 in Blounts Creek, North Carloina, d: 15 Feb 2002 in Blounts Creek, North Carloina

..............6 Gerture Keyes b: 1921 in Blounts Creek, North Carolina

+ Thelma Mooree b: Blounts Creek, N.C, d: Blounts Creek, N.C

..............6 Heretford Keyes b: 1924 in Blounts Creek, North Carloina, d: 21 Aug 1948 in Blounts Creek, North Carolina

..............6 Iola Keyes b: 28 Mar 1927 in Blounts Creek, North Carolina, d: 20 Apr 1927 in Blounts Creek, North Carolina

............5 Elizabeth Keyes b: 1884 in Blounts Creek, North Carloina, d: Blounts Creek, North Carolina`

+ Phillip Keyes b: 1886 in Blounts Creek, North Carolina, d: 05 Mar 1975 in Blounts Creek, North Carolina

..............6 Lloyd Keyes b: 1908 in Blounts Creek, North Carolina, d: 14 Jan 1947 in Blounts Creek, North Carolina

..............6 Kessiah Keyes b: 01 Jan 1909 in Blounts Creek, North Carolina, d: 19 Oct 1988 in Blounts Creek, North Carolina

..............6 Joseph Keyes b: 1911 in Blounts Creek, North Carolina, d: Blounts Creek, North Carolina

............5 Orlando Keys b: 1885 in Blounts Creek, North Carolina, d: 18 Oct 1966 in Blounts Creek, North Carolina

+ [unknown spouse]

..............6 Jessie Keys

+ John Henry Smith b: 1911 in Blounts Creek, North Carolina, d: 1989 in Beaufort County North Carolina

.................7 Coreen Smith b: 1934 in Blounts Creek, North Carolina

+ Archie D (Kelly) Moore b: 1930 in Blounts Creek, North Carolina

....................8 Elaine Moore b: Blounts Creek, North Carolina

....................8 Archie Moore b: Blounts Creek, North Carolina

....................8 Eddie Moore b: Blounts Creek, North Carolina

....................8 Stevie Moore b: Blounts Creek, North Carolina

....................8 Kelvin Moore b: Blounts Creek, North Carolina

....................8 Charlene Moore b: Blounts Creek, North Carolina

+ [unknown spouse]

..............6 Earl Lee Keyes b: 1922 in Blounts Creek, North Carloina

+ Benjaline Oden b: 1921, d: 2002 in Blounts Creek, N.C
...........7 Melvin E Keyes b: 05 Sep 1940
...........7 Peggy L Oden b: 03 Mar 1949
...........7 Beatrice Oden b: 07 Jun 1950
+ Carrie Stilley b: 1890 in Edward, N.C, d: 29 Jun 1946 in Blounts Creek, North Carolina
...........6 Booker T Keys b: 31 Mar 1913 in Blounts Creek, North Carolina, d: 04 Apr 1983 in Washington. N.C
+ Grace Moore b: 1914 in Blounts Creek, North Carolina, d: 18 Jul 1980 in Washington. N.C
...........7 Ashley Keyes b: 15 Oct 1936 in Blounts Creek, North Carolina, d: 24 Apr 2001 in Blounts Creek, North Carolina
...........7 Bunyon Keys b: 23 Feb 1943 in Blounts Creek, North Carolina
+ Dorothy M Florence b: 13 Aug 1946 in Shreveport, La, m: 09 Feb 1965 in Shreveport, La
...............8 Yulonda P Keys b: 17 Apr 1966 in Wiesbaden, Ger
+ Wayne Boston
...................9 Andrew D Lindsey b: 20 Aug 1987 in Forth Worth, Tx
...............8 Michael O Keys b: 20 Jul 1967 in Wiesbaden, Ger
...........7 Booker T Jr Keyes b: 23 Sep 1945 in Blounts Creek, North Carolina
...........7 Vincent A Keys b: 07 Dec 1946 in Blounts Creek, North Carolina

+ Nolan Beth Scott b: 1955, m: 1976 in Merced, Ca
...............8 Vincent Jr Keys b: 1976 in Merced, Ca
...............8 Vensus C Keys b: 1979 in Merced, Ca
...............8 Victor T Keys b: 1981 in Forth Worth, Tx
...........7 Vance Keyes b: 20 Mar 1948 in Blounts Creek, North Carolina
...........7 Nancy G Keyes b: 20 Mar 1948 in Blounts Creek, North Carolina

............7 William Oakley Keys b: Blounts Creek, North Carolina

............6 Lula M Keys b: Apr 1914 in Blounts Creek, North Carolina, d: 06 Feb 1987 in Norfolk, Va

+ Golden C Hudgins b: 16 Sep 1912, d: 26 Mar 1987 in Norfolk, Va

............7 Thelma Hudgins

............6 Jessie M Keys b: 1916 in Blounts Creek, North Carolina, d: 13 Mar 1993

............6 Orlanda Keys II b: 1919 in Blounts Creek, North Carolina, d: 10 Aug 1934 in Blounts Creek, North Carolina

............6 Earl Lee Keyes b: 1922 in Blounts Creek, North Carloina

+ Benjaline Oden b: 1921, d: 2002 in Blounts Creek, N.C

............7 Melvin E Keyes b: 05 Sep 1940

............7 Peggy L Oden b: 03 Mar 1949

............7 Beatrice Oden b: 07 Jun 1950

............6 Earlice Keys b: Blounts Creek, North Carolina, d: 20 Jan 1923 in Edward, N.C

..........5 Grace Keyes b: 15 Feb 1891 in Blounts Creek, North Carloina, d: 21 Sep 1919 in Blounts Creek, North Carloina

+ James A Moore b: 16 Dec 1896 in Bonnenton, North Carolina, d: Blounts Creek, North Carolina

............6 Oswald K Moore b: 1919 in Blounts Creek, North Carolina, d: Alliance, North Carolina

........4 Jane Keyes b: 1853 in Blounts Creek, North Carloina, d: Blounts Creek, North Carloina

+ James M Moore b: 1835 in Blounts Creek, N.C, d: Blounts Creek, N.C

..........5 William Moore b: 1855 in Blounts Creek, N.C, d: Blounts Creek, N.C

+ [unknown spouse]

............6 Elijah Moore b: 1895 in Blounts Creek, North Carolina, d: 1956 in Blounts Creek, North Carloina

+ Angline Moore b: 1899 in Blounts Creek, North Carolina, d: 1987 in Beaufort County North Carolina

............5 Henry Moore b: 1857 in Blounts Creek, N.C, d: Blounts Creek, N.C

............5 Isreal Moore b: 1864 in Blounts Creek, N.C, d: Blounts Creek, N.C

............5 Mary Moore b: 1866 in Blounts Creek, N.C, d: Blounts Creek, N.C

............5 Bannon Moore b: 1868 in Blounts Creek, N.C, d: 1925 in Blounts Creek, N.C

+ Margaret Blango b: 1863 in Blounts Creek, North Carolina, d: 1927 in Blounts Creek, North Carolina

...............6 Betsy Moore b: 1894 in Blounts Creek, North Carolina, d: 1977 in Blounts Creek, North Carolina

+ Jesse (Blango) Moore b: 1891 in Blounts Creek, North Carolina, d: 1960 in Blounts Creek, North Carolina

..................7 Geneva Moore b: 1913 in Blounts Creek, North Carolina

..................7 Mahue Moore b: 1918 in Blounts Creek, North Carolina, d: 1987 in New Bern, Craven, North Carolina, USA

+ Edna Roberson b: 1921 in Beaufort Bridge, Kerry, Ireland, d: 1998 in Beaufort County North Carolina

......................8 Ivesta Moore b: Blounts Creek, North Carolina, d: Beaufort County North Carolina

......................8 Marvin E Moore b: Blounts Creek, North Carolina

...............6 James E Moore b: 1894 in Blounts Creek, North Carolina, d: 1935 in Blounts Creek, North Carolina

+ Cora I Williams b: 1900 in Beaufort County North Carolina, d: 1986 in New York, New York, New York, USA

..................7 Bannon Moore b: 1921 in Blounts Creek, North Carolina, d: 1976 in Blounts Creek, North Carolina

+ Idessa b: 1923 in Blounts Creek, North Carolina, d: 1994 in Beaufort County North Carolina

......................8 Dorothy Moore b: Blounts Creek, North Carolina

................8 Bannon Moore Jr. b: Blounts Creek, North Carolina
................8 Zachariaj Moore b: Blounts Creek, North Carolina
................8 Bessie Moore b: Blounts Creek, North Carolina
................8 Terry D Moore b: Blounts Creek, North Carolina
................8 Donald D Moore b: Blounts Creek, North Carolina
................8 Clyde R Moore b: Blounts Creek, North Carolina
................8 Samuel Moore b: Blounts Creek, North Carolina
................8 Leroy Moore b: Blounts Creek, North Carolina
............7 Archie D (Kelly) Moore b: 1930 in Blounts Creek, North Carolina
+ Coreen Smith b: 1934 in Blounts Creek, North Carolina
................8 Elaine Moore b: Blounts Creek, North Carolina
................8 Archie Moore b: Blounts Creek, North Carolina
................8 Eddie Moore b: Blounts Creek, North Carolina
................8 Stevie Moore b: Blounts Creek, North Carolina
................8 Kelvin Moore b: Blounts Creek, North Carolina
................8 Charlene Moore b: Blounts Creek, North Carolina
+ [unknown spouse]
............6 Elizabeth Moore b: 1897 in Blounts Creek, North Carolina, d: 1951 in Beaufort County North Carolina
+ Josephus Keys b: 1889 in Blounts Creek, North Carolina, d: 1967 in Beaufort County North Carolina
............7 Murphy Keys b: 1923 in Blounts Creek, North Carolina, d: 2013 in North Carolina
+ Annie L Peacock b: 1925 in Beaufort County North Carolina, d: 2011 in Beaufort County North Carolina
................8 Ruffin Keys b: Blounts Creek, North Carolina
................8 Charles D Keys b: Blounts Creek, North Carolina
............7 Virginia D Keys b: 1925 in Blounts Creek, North Carolina, d: 2010 in Beaufort County North Carolina
+ James A Moore b: 1922 in Beaufort County North Carolina, d: 2009 in Washington, D.C.
................8 James C Moore b: Blounts Creek, North Carolina
................8 Edward P Moore b: Blounts Creek, North Carolina

................8 Kenneth L Moore b: Blounts Creek, North Carolina
................8 Claude A Moore b: Blounts Creek, North Carolina
................8 William D Moore b: Blounts Creek, North Carolina
................8 Clarence E Moore b: Blounts Creek, North Carolina
................8 Arthur M Moore b: Blounts Creek, North Carolina
..........5 Moore Moore b: 1869 in Blounts Creek, N.C, d: Blounts Creek, N.C
......3 Grace Keyes b: 1820 in Craven County North Carolina, d: 1857 in Blounts Creek, North Carolina
......3 Mary Ann Green b: 1821 in Craven County North Carolina
......3 Wiliam Keys Jr. b: 1821 in Craven County North Carolina
+ Visa Keys m: 29 Dec 1845 in Craven County, North Carolina
.........4 William Keys b: 1846 in Craven County North Carolina
.........4 Charles Keys b: 1847 in Craven County North Carolina; Caroline
+ Tamar Bell b: 1850 in Craven County, North Carolina, m: 26 Mar 1871, d: Bef. 1915 in Craven County, North Carolina
............5 Carrie C Keys b: 1871
............5 Charity Keys b: 1872 in Craven County, North Carolina
............5 Ellen Keys b: 1874 in Craven County, North Carolina
............5 Amandia Keys b: 1876 in Craven County, North Carolina
............5 Francis Keys b: 1879 in Craven County, North Carolina
............5 Charles Keys Jr. b: 1880 in Craven County, North Carolina

............5 Florence Keys b: 1882 in Craven County North Carolina
............5 Mary J Keys b: 1883 in Craven County, North Carolina
............5 Augusta Keys b: 1886 in Craven County, North Carolina
............5 Anita Keys b: 1888 in Craven County, North Carolina
............5 Lola Keys b: 1890 in Craven County, North Carolina
............5 Sadie Keys b: 1893 in Craven County, North Carolina
............5 Bertha Keys b: 1893 in Craven County, North Carolina
............5 Bessie F Keys b: 1899 in Craven County North Carolina

............5 Mattie Keys b: 1899
+ Martha Dickerson Blunt b: 1865 in Pamlico, North Carolina, USA, m: 07 Mar 1915 in Pamlico
............5 Jefferson Blunt b: 1910 in Pamlico, North Carolina, USA
............5 Marthy Blunt b: 1914 in Pamlico, North Carolina, USA
............5 Earnest Blunt b: 1915 in Pamlico, North Carolina, USA
............5 Bety Blunt b: 1918
............5 Maddie Blunt
.........4 Caroline Keys b: 1850 in Craven County North Carolina
.........4 Laura Keys b: 1853 in Craven County, North Carolina
.........4 Isaac Keys b: 1856 in Craven County North Carolina
.........4 Salix Keys b: 1858 in Craven County North Carolina
...2 Lucy Keys b: Abt. 1775 in B lountsa Creek, North Carolina
+ [unknown spouse]
......3 John Keys b: 1813 in Blounts Creek, North Carolina
...2 Clary (Charity) Keys b: Abt. 1776 in Blounts Creek, North Carolina
+ [unknown spouse]
......3 Noah Keys b: Abt. 1795 in Blounts Creek, North Carolina
+ [unknown spouse]
.........4 Noah (Jr) Keys b: Abt. 1815 in Morven, Anson, North Carolina
+ [unknown spouse]
............5 Mary Keys b: 1812 in Morven, Anson, North Carolina, d: 1870 in Morven, Anson, North Carolina
+ Dove Teal b: Abt. 1810 in Morven, Anson, North Carolina
............5 Sara Keys b: 1824 in Morven, Anson, North Carolina
+ [unknown spouse]
...............6 s
............5 Lydia Keys b: 1826 in Morven, Anson, North Carolina
...2 Silvy Keys b: Abt. 1780 in B lountsa Creek, North Carolina
+ [unknown spouse]
......3 Zachariah Keys b: 1815 in Blounts Creek, North Carolina
+ [unknown spouse]

.........4 Mary Keys b: 1832 in Beaufort County North Carolina
.........4 William Keys b: 1838 in Beaufort County North Carolina
.........4 Octavia Keys b: 1856 in Beaufort County North Carolina
.........4 Elizabeth Keys b: 1859 in Beaufort County North Carolina
...2 Wyatt Keys b: Abt. 1780 in Blounts Creek, North Carolina
+ Jeliky Rhodes b: Abt. 1790 in Craven County, North Carolina
...2 Malachi Keys b: Abt. 1784 in Blounts Creek, North Carolina
+ [unknown spouse]
......3 Malachi (Jr.) Keys b: 1810 in Blounts Creek, North Carolina
...2 Penny Keys b: Abt. 1786 in B lountsa Creek, North Carolina
...2 Mary Keys b: Abt. 1789 in Blounts Creek, North Carolina, d: 1825 in Beaufort County North Carolina
+ [unknown spouse]
...2 Amy Keys b: 1769 in Blounts Creek, Beaufort, North Carolina, USA
+ Willioughby Moore b: 1773 in Blounts Creek, Beaufort, North Carolina, USA, d: Bef. 1850 in Blounts Creek, Beaufort, North Carolina, USA

......3 Mary A Keys b: 1823 in Blounts Creek, Beaufort, North Carolina, USA
...2 Nancy Keys b: 1771
...2 Sally Keys b: 1773 in Blounts Creek, Beaufort, North Carolina, USA
+ [unknown spouse]
......3 John Keys b: 1796 in Blounts Creek, Beaufort, North Carolina, USA
+ Mary Keys b: 1812 in Blounts Creek, Beaufort, North Carolina, USA
.........4 Kennedy Keys b: 1832 in Blounts Creek, Beaufort, North Carolina, USA
.........4 John Keys Jr b: 1834 in Blounts Creek, Beaufort, North Carolina, USA
+ Nancy Keys

............5 Mary Keys b: 1854 in Blounts Creek, Beaufort, North Carolina, USA

............5 Bannon Keys b: 1857 in Blounts Creek, Beaufort, North Carolina, USA

+ Peggy A Moore b: 1865 in Blounts Creek, Beaufort, North Carolina, USA, d: 1944 in Beaufort County North Carolina

...............6 David Keys b: 1900 in Beaufort County North Carolina, d: 1957 in Beaufort County North Carolina

...............6 Lacy Keys b: 1901 in Beaufort County North Carolina

...............6 Tinsey Keys b: 1902 in Beaufort County North Carolina

...............6 Sussie Keys b: 1907 in Beaufort C

...............6 Simon Keys b: 1911 in Beaufort County North Carolina

.........4 Pheraby Keys b: 1836 in Blounts Creek, Beaufort, North Carolina, USA

.........4 William Keys b: 1837 in Blounts Creek, North Carolina

.........4 David Keys b: 1839 in Blounts Creek, Beaufort, North Carolina, USA

.........4 Joseph Keys b: 1841 in Blounts Creek, Beaufort, North Carolina, USA

.........4 Isiah Keys b: 1843 in Blounts Creek, Beaufort, North Carolina, USA

...2 William Keys b: 1774 in Blounts Creek, Beaufort, North Carolina, USA

+ Mary Thornton b: 1780 in Craven County North Carolina

......3 Lydia Keys b: 1805 in Craven County North Carolina, d: Bef. 1870 in Blounts Creek, Beaufort, North Carolina, USA

+ Giles Moore b: 1792 in Blounts Creek, North Carloina, d: Blounts Creek, North Carloina

.........4 Martha P Moore b: 1831 in Blounts Creek, Beaufort, North Carolina, USA, d: 1915 in Blounts Creek, Beaufort, North Carolina, USA

+ James H Moore b: 1826, d: 1867 in Blounts Creek, North Carolina

......3 Grace Keys b: 1820 in Craven County North Carolina, d: 1857 in Blounts Creek, Beaufort, North Carolina, USA

......3 Mary Ann Green b: 1820 in Craven County North Carolina

......3 William Keys Jr. b: 1821 in Craven County North Carolina, d: Bef. 1860 in Craven County North Carolina

+ Visa Keys b: 1821 in Craven County North Carolina, d: Bef. 1870 in Craven County North Carolina

.........4 William Keys b: 1846 in Craven County North Carolina

...2 Lucy Keys b: 1775 in Blounts Creek, Beaufort, North Carolina, USA, d: Bef. 1870 in Martin County, North Carolina

+ [unknown spouse]

......3 John Keys b: 1813 in Blounts Creek, Beaufort, North Carolina, USA

+ Emerline Grice b: 1836 in Martin County, North Carolina

...2 Clary Keys b: 1776 in Blounts Creek, Beaufort, North Carolina, USA

...2 Silvy Keys b: 1780 in Blounts Creek, Beaufort, North Carolina, USA

...2 Silvy Keys b: 1780 in Blounts Creek, Beaufort, North Carolina, USA, d: Bef. 1870 in Beaufort County North Carolina

+ [unknown spouse]

......3 Zachariah Keys b: 1814 in Blounts Creek, Beaufort, North Carolina, USA

+ Mary Keys b: 1823 in Beaufort County North Carolina

...2 Waytt Keys b: 1780 in Blounts Creek, North Carolina

+ Jeliky Rhodes m: 1832 in Craven County North Carolina

...2 Malachi Keys b: 1784 in Blounts Creek, Beaufort, North Carolina, USA

...2 Penny Keys b: 1786 in Blounts Creek, Beaufort, North Carolina, USA

...2 Mary Keys b: 1789

+ [unknown spouse]

......3 Lacy Keys b: 1812 in Blounts Creek, Beaufort, North Carolina, USA

......3 Lacy Keys b: 1812 in Blounts Creek, Beaufort, North Carolina, USA

......3 John Keys b: 1815 in Blounts Creek, Beaufort, North Carolina, USA

......3 John Keyes b: 1815 in Blounts Creek, North Carolina

+ Francis Keyes b: Abt. 1820 in Blounts Creek, North Carolina

.........4 John Keyes b: 1843 in Blounts Creek, North Carolina

.........4 Zachariah Keyes b: 1845 in Blounts Creek, North Carolina

+ [unknown spouse]

............5 Bannon Keyes b: Chocowinity

+ Peggy A Moore b: 1857 in Blounts Creek, North Carolina

.........4 Southey Keyes b: 1847 in Blounts Creek, North Carolina

.........4 Lewis Keyes b: 1849

......3 Lewis Keys b: 1818 in Blounts Creek, Beaufort, North Carolina, USA, d: 1875 in Martin County, North Carolina

+ Sara Moore b: 1826 in Blounts Creek, North Carolina, d: 1932 in Hyde County, North Carolina

.........4 Nancy Keys b: 1847 in Blounts Creek, Beaufort, North Carolina, USA, d: 1918

+ John Taper b: 1840 in Martin County, North Carolina, m: 1860 in Martín Colman, Buenos Aires, Argentina

............5 Isaac Taper b: 1865

............5 John T Taper b: 1866 in Martin County, North Carolina, d: 1919 in Martin County, North Carolina

+ Katie H James b: 1871 in Martin County, North Carolina, d: 1937 in Martin County, North Carolina

...............6 Sophia Taper b: 1882 in Martín Colman, Buenos Aires, Argentina

...............6 Lena Taper b: 1890 in Martin County, North Carolina, d: 1939 in Martin County, North Carolina

+ Solomon Hodge b: 1882 in Martin County, North Carolina, m: 1887 in Martin County, North Carolina, d: 1933 in Martín Colman, Buenos Aires, Argentina

..................7 Elton Hodge b: 1905 in Martin County, North Carolina

..................7 Vernice Hodge b: 1910 in Martin County, North Carolina

..................7 Horace Hodge b: 1912 in Martin County, North Carolina

..................7 Alexander Hodge b: 1917 in Martin County, North Carolina

..................7 Elbert Hodge b: 1919 in Martin County, North Carolina

..................7 Bradford Hodge b: 1920 in Martiin CXounty, North Carolina

..................7 Solmon Hodge b: 1922 in Martín Colman, Buenos Aires, Argentina

..................7 Kathrine Hodge b: 1924 in Martin County, North Carolina

..................7 Calvin Hodge b: 1927 in Martin County, North Carolina

...............6 Johnnie Taper b: 1892 in Martin County, North Carolina, d: 1919 in Martin County, North Carolina

+ Indiana Boston b: 1894 in Martin County, North Carolina, d: 1985 in Martin County, North Carolina

...............6 Ada Taper b: 1893 in Martin County, North Carolina, d: 1974 in Goldsboro, Wayne, North Carolina, USA

...............6 Clarence Taper b: 1896 in Martin County, North Carolina, d: 1951 in Martin County, North Carolina

+ Mittie Boston b: 1896 in Martin County, North Carolina, m: 1917 in Martin County, North Carolina, d: 1974 in Rocky Mount, Edgecombe, North Carolina, USA

..................7 Luris Taper b: 1920 in Martin County, North Carolina

..................7 Heles M Taper b: 1924 in Martin County, North Carolina

..................7 Tharix Taper b: 1932 in Martin County, North Carolina

..................7 Claris Taper b: 1935 in Martin County, North Carolina

............6 Katie Taper b: 1899 in Martin County, North Carolina, d: 1937 in Martin County, North Carolina

............6 Gladys Taper b: 1901 in Martin County, North Carolina

+ Abraham Pierce b: 1897 in Plymouth, Washington, North Carolina, USA, d: 1952 in Plymouth, Washington, North Carolina, USA

...............7 Johnathan Pierce b: 1918 in Plymouth, Washington, North Carolina, USA

...............7 William Pierce b: 1920 in Plymouth, Washington, North Carolina, USA

...............7 Leon Pierce b: 1922 in Plymouth, Washington, North Carolina, USA

+ Frank Brooks b: 1860 in Martin County, North Carolina, d: 1907 in Martin County, North Carolina

.........4 William H Keys b: 1853 in Martin County, North Carolina

.........4 Christopher C Keys b: 1855 in Martín Colman, Buenos Aires, Argentina, d: 1936 in Martin County, North Carolina

+ Sophia Peelee b: 1875 in Martin County, North Carolina, d: 1892 in Martin County, North Carolina

............5 Charles Keys b: 1859 in Martin County, North Carolina

+ Diane Riggs b: 1852 in Edgecombe, Edgecombe, North Carolina, USA, m: 1912

............6 Spier Keys b: 1870 in Martin County, North Carolina, d: 1916 in Martin County, North Carolina

+ Sara Knight b: 1880 in Martin County, North Carolina, m: 1900, d: 1938 in Martin County, North Carolina; bbbb 8

+ Alberta Griffin b: 1892

............5 James Cedon Keys b: 1884 in Martin County, North Carolina, d: 1913 in Boston, Mass.

............5 Christopher F Keys b: 1888 in Martin County, North Carolina, d: 1919 in Martín Colman, Buenos Aires, Argentina

+ Elizabeth Powell b: 1890 in Martin County, North Carolina

............6 Mary Marie Keys b: 1911 in Martin County, North Carolina, d: 1987 in Martin County, North Carolina

+ Jasper Smith b: 1910 in Martin County, North Carolina, d: 1897 in Martin County, North Carolina

..................7 Annie Smith b: 1931 in Martin County, North Carolina

..................7 Willie Smith b: 1933 in Martin County, North Carolina

..................7 Doris Smith b: 1933 in Martin County, North Carolina

..................7 Beatrice Smith b: 1936 in Martin County, North Carolina

..................7 Joseph Smith b: 1939 in Martin County, North Carolina, d: 2002 in Martin County, North Carolina

............6 Christen Keys b: 1914 in Martin County, North Carolina, d: 2000 in Pitt County. North Carolina

+ Matthew Lewis b: 1910 in Hertford, North Carolina, USA, d: 2009 in Pitt County. North Carolina

..................7 Matthew H Lewis Jr b: 1935 in Pitt County. North Carolina

..................7 James R Lewis b: 1939 in Pitt County. North Carolina

..................7 Edward E Lewis b: 1941 in Pitt County. North Carolina

..................7 Elizabeth A Lewis b: 1946 in Pitt County. North Carolina

..........5 Sadie Keys b: 1890 in Martin County, North Carolina, d: 1927 in Martin County, North Carolina

+ Jobe Daniel b: 1885 in Martin County, North Carolina, m: 1906 in Martin County, North Carolina, d: 1911 in Martin County, North Carolina

............6 Sophia E Daniel b: 1908 in Martin County, North Carolina

............6 James R Daniel b: 1909 in Martin County, North Carolina

............6 Samuel L Daniel b: 1911 in Martin County, North Carolina

+ Henry Moore b: 1884 in Martin County, North Carolina, m: 1912 in Martin County, North Carolina

............6 Lillie B Moore b: 1914 in Martin County, North Carolina

............6 Charley Moore b: 1915 in Martin County, North Carolina

............6 Luther Moore b: 1917 in Martin County, North Carolina

............6 Ailaca G Moore b: 1918 in Martin County, North Carolina, d: 1965 in Martin County, North Carolina

............6 George Moore b: 1920 in Martin County, North Carolina, d: 1986 in Martín Colman, Buenos Aires, Argentina

............6 Granville Moore b: 1922 in Martin County, North Carolina, d: 1972 in Martin County, North Carolina

............6 Mary A Moore b: 1923 in Martin County, North Carolina, d: 2008 in Martin County, North Carolina

+ Thadious Woolard m: 1940

...............7 Wesley Woolard b: 1948 in Martin County, North Carolina

...............7 Richard Woolard b: 1949 in Martin County, North Carolina

...............7 Doris Woolard b: 1953 in Martin County, North Carolina

...............7 Douglas Woolard b: 1956 in Martin County, North Carolina

..........5 Mamie Keys b: 1897 in Martin County, North Carolina, d: 1925 in Martin County, North Carolin

+ Mack D Woolard b: 1887 in Plymouth, Washngton County, North Carolina, m: 1910, d: 1975 in Plymouth, Washngton County, North Carolina

................6 Crystal Woolard b: 1914 in Plymouth, Washngton County, North Carolina, d: 1972 in Washington County, North Carolina

................6 Joseph Woolard b: 1916 in Washington County, North Carolina, d: 1979 in Washington, D.C.

+ Lucy Eillison b: 1920 in North Carolina, USA, d: 1920 in North Carolina, USA

................6 Dorothy E Woolard b: 1920 in Plymouth, Washngton County, North Carolina, d: 2003 in Washington County, North Carolina

................6 Mack K Woolard b: 1927 in Plymouth, Washngton County, North Carolina, d: 1927 in Plymouth, Washngton County, North Carolina

............5 Rosa F Keys b: 1897 in Martin County, North Carolina, d: 1965 in Martin County, North Carolina

+ George L Haridson b: 1897 in Martin County, North Carolina, m: 1923, d: 1959 in Martin County, North Carolina

................6 Nathaniel Haridson b: 1924

+ Quennie E Woolard b: 1936 in Martin County, North Carolina

................6 Mildred Haridson b: 1929 in Martin County, North Carolina

................6 Majory Haridson b: 1934 in Martin County, North Carolina

+ Lonnie H Moore b: 1919 in Martin County, North Carolina, d: 1987 in Martin County, North Carolina

............5 Rudella Keys b: 1903 in Martin County, North Carolina, d: 1937 in Martin County, North Carolina

+ William Boston b: 1898 in Martin County, North Carolina, m: 1928, d: 1976 in Martin County, North Carolina

................6 Fredick Boston b: 1934 in Martin County, North Carolina

................6 Roscoe Boston b: 1935 in Martin County, North Carolina

+ Florence Gaylord b: 1867 in Martin County, North Carolina, m: 1896, d: 1945 in Martin County, North Carolina

............5 Lena C Keys b: 1900 in Martin County, North Carolina
+ Andrew Jones b: 1897 in Martin County, North Carolina, m: 1920
...............6 Mary Jones b: 1924 in Martin County, North Carolina
...............6 Katlapie Jones b: 1924 in Martín Colman, Buenos Aires, Argentina
...............6 Omar Jones b: 1928 in Martin County, North Carolina
...............6 Haywood Jones b: 1928 in Martin County, North Carolina
...............6 Carlton Jones b: 1936 in Martin County, North Carolina
.........4 Caesar Keys b: 1857 in Martin County, North Carolina
.........4 Charles Keys b: 1859 in Martin County, North Carolina
+ Diane Riggs b: 1852 in Edgecombe, Edgecombe, North Carolina, USA, m: 1912
............5 Spier Keys b: 1870 in Martin County, North Carolina, d: 1916 in Martin County, North Carolina
+ Sara Knight b: 1880 in Martin County, North Carolina, m: 1900, d: 1938 in Martin County, North Carolina; bbbb 8

+ Alberta Griffin b: 1892
.........4 Robert Keys b: 1860 in Martin County, North Carolina, d: 1933 in Martin County, North Carolina
+ Harriet Moore b: 1862 in Martín Colman, Buenos Aires, Argentina, m: 1893
............5 Sadie Keys b: 1893 in Martin County, North Carolina, d: 1931 in Holy Neck, Nansemond, Virginia, USA
+ James Ruffin b: 1899 in Bertie, North Carolina, USA, m: 1921, d: 1984 in Buffalo, Erie, New York, USA
...............6 William Ruffin b: 1922 in Holy Neck, Nansemond, Virginia, USA
...............6 James Ruffin b: 1926 in Holy Neck, Nansemond, Virginia, USA
...............6 Levy Ruffin b: 1929 in Holy Neck, Nansemond, Virginia, USA

............5 Courtney Keys b: 1894 in Martín Colman, Buenos Aires, Argentina

............5 Lovey F Keys b: 1896 in Martin County, North Carolina

............5 Bessie Keys b: 1899 in Martin County, North Carolina

............5 Isaac Keys b: 1900 in Martin County, North Carolina

............5 Lizette Keys b: 1902 in Martin County, North Carolina, d: 1932 in Martin County, North Carolina

............5 Pearlie M Keys b: 1907 in Martin County, North Carolina

............5 Harriet Keys b: 1909 in Martin County, North Carolina

.........4 Kizziah Keys b: 1866 in Martin County, North Carolina, d: 1918 in Martin County, North Carolina

+ [unknown spouse]

............5 Lewis Keyes b: 1886 in Martin County, North Carolina, d: 1963 in Martin County, North Carolin

+ Sallie Pierce b: 1899 in Martin County, North Carolina, d: 1949 in Martin County, North Carolina

...............6 Mamie Keyes b: 1908 in Martin County, North Carolina

...............6 James Keyes b: 1910 in Martin County, North Carolina

...............6 Tuirthy Keyes b: 1912 in Martin County, North Carolina

...............6 Elijah Keyes b: 1914 in Martin County, North Carolina

...............6 Hubert Keyes b: 1917 in Martin County, North Carolina

...............6 Austrilla Keyes b: 1919 in Martin County, North Carolina

...............6 Howard Keyes b: 1921 in Martin County, North Carolina

............5 Hattie Keyes b: 1892 in Martín Colman, Buenos Aires, Argentina

+ Rufus Hodge b: 1879 in Martin County, North Carolina, m: 1909

...............6 Alfred Hodge b: 1902 in Martin County, North Carolina

............6 Felton Hodge b: 1902 in Martin County, North Carolina
............6 Pearly Hodge b: 1903 in Martin County, North Carolina
..........5 Mollie Keyes b: 1895 in Martín Colman, Buenos Aires, Argentina, d: 1964 in Martín Colman, Buenos Aires, Argentina
+ James Matthew Peierce b: 1892 in Martin County, North Carolina
............6 Walter Peierce b: 1914 in Martin County, North Carolina
............6 Edmond Peierce b: 1919 in Martin County, North Carolina
............6 Bessie Peierce b: 1924 in Martin County, North Carolina
............6 Irdell Peierce b: 1925 in Martin County, North Carolina
............6 Alva Peierce b: 1927 in Martin County, North Carolina
............6 John Peierce b: 1928 in Martin County, North Carolina
............6 Hoover Peierce b: 1930 in Martin County, North Carolina
........4 Ivory Keys b: 1868 in Martin County, North Carolina, d: 1932 in Hyde County, North Carolina
+ Margaret E Boston b: 1874 in Martin County, North Carolina, m: 1893, d: 1910 in Hyde County, North Carolina
..........5 Benjamin F Keys b: 1893 in Hyde County, North Carolina, d: 1939 in Martin County, North Carolina
+ Beartrice F Smith b: 1897 in Martin County, North Carolina, d: 1937 in Martin County, North Carolina
............6 Maggie Keys b: 1916 in Martin County, North Carolina
............6 Elmer Keys b: 1918 in Martin County, North Carolina
............6 Solomon Keys b: 1920 in Martin County, North Carolina

............6 Benjamin Keys b: 1922 in Martin County, North Carolina

............6 Christine Keys b: 1923 in Martin County, North Carolina

..........5 Walter R Keys b: 1896 in Hyde County, North Carolina, d: 1985 in Martin County, North Carolina

+ Minnia G Hill b: 1901 in Martin County, North Carolina, m: 1916, d: 2005 in Brooklyn, New York

............6 Balligh Keys b: 1922 in Martin County, North Carolina
............6 Odelsie Keys b: 1924 in Martin County, North Carolina
............6 Goletha Keys b: 1928 in Martin County, North Carolina
............6 Nina M Keys b: 1931 in Martin County, North Carolina
............6 Novealle Keys b: 1934

..........5 Dora Keys b: 1899 in Hyde County, North Carolina, d: 1999 in Fort Washington, Prince George's, Maryland, USA

+ Wilford Staton b: 1898 in Martin County, North Carolina, m: 1919

............6 Moses Staton b: 1921 in Martin County, North Carolina
............6 Annie L Staton b: 1922 in Martin County, North Carolina
............6 Bradford Staton b: 1923 in Martin County, North Carolina
............6 John D Staton b: 1924 in Martin County, North Carolina
............6 Oscar L Staton b: 1929 in Martin County, North Carolina
............6 Larrengay Staton b: 1930 in Martin County, North Carolina
............6 Onward Staton b: 1933 in Martin County, North Carolina
............6 Flora J Staton b: 1935 in Martin County, North Carolina

+ Nancy D Barber b: 1893 in Martin County, North Carolina, d: 1895 in Martín Colman, Buenos Aires, Argentina

............5 William S Keys b: 1904 in Hyde County, North Carolina, d: 1962 in Washington County, North Carolina

+ Nancy E James b: 1903 in Martin County, North Carolina, m: 1921, d: 1985 in Martin County, North Carolina

...............6 Milford Keys b: 1922 in Martin County, North Carolina

...............6 Linwood Keys b: 1926 in Martín Colman, Buenos Aires, Argentina

...............6 William Keys b: 1929 in Martín Colman, Buenos Aires, Argentina

............5 Wilbert D Keys b: 1913 in Hyde County, North Carolina

............5 James L Keys b: 1914 in Hyde County, North Carolina, d: 1976 in North Carolina

+ Hazel Credle b: 1915 in Martin County, North Carolina, m: 1935, d: 2002 in Brooklyn, New York

............5 James H Keys b: 1914 in Hyde County, North Carolina

............5 Ivory J Keys b: 1918 in Hyde County, North Carolina, d: 1963

+ Viola Ward b: 1929 in Martin County, North Carolina, m: 1953, d: 2006 in Martin County, North Carolina

............5 Luellen Keys b: 1920 in Hyde County, North Carolina, d: 1984 in Martin County, North Carolina

+ Addie L James b: 1922 in Martin County, North Carolina, m: 1927, d: 2000 in Martin County, North Carolina

............5 Benjamin L Keys b: 1925 in Hyde County, North Carolina, d: 1992 in Hyde County, North Carolina

............5 Mary J Keys b: 1927 in Hyde County, North Carolina

............5 Roosevelt Keys b: 1927 in Hyde County, North Carolina, d: 1922 in Hyde County, North Carolina

.........4 Frank J Keys b: 1869 in Martin County, North Carolina, d: 1915 in Martin County, North Carolina

.........4 Sara E Keys b: 1873 in Martin County, North Carolina, d: 1938

+ Benji Boston b: 1867 in Martin County, North Carolina, m: 1891

............5 Willis A Boston b: 1892 in Martin County, North Carolina, d: 1960 in Martín Colman, Buenos Aires, Argentina

+ Essie Barton b: 1894 in Martin County, North Carolina

...............6 Nathaniel Boston b: 1914 in Martin County, North Carolina

...............6 JamesH Boston b: 1916 in Martin County, North Carolina

...............6 Annie G Boston b: 1917 in Martin County, North Carolina

...............6 William Boston b: 1917 in Martin County, North Carolina

...............6 Minnie J Boston b: 1921 in Martin County, North Carolina

...............6 Mary E Boston b: 1923 in Martin County, North Carolina

...............6 Albert Boston b: 1925 in Martin County, North Carolina

............5 Dollie Boston b: 1895 in Martín Colman, Buenos Aires, Argentina, d: 1953 in Martin County, North Carolina

+ Willie b: 1893 in Martin County, North Carolina, d: 1932 in Martin County, North Carolina

...............6 Jasper Willie b: 1914 in Martín Colman, Buenos Aires, Argentina, d: 1930 in Martin County, North Carolina

...............6 Nacy Willie b: 1914 in Martin County, North Carolina, d: 1960 in Martin County, North Carolina

...............6 Bernice Willie b: 1916 in Martin County, North Carolina, d: 1920 in Martin County, North Carolina

...............6 Allie B Willie b: 1920 in Martin County, North Carolina

...............6 Vinonia Willie b: 1922 in Martin County, North Carolina, d: 1994 in Martin County, North Carolina

............5 Manford A Boston b: 1899 in Martin County, North Carolina

+ Edith Pitman b: 1898 in Martin County, North Carolina, m: 1919 in Martin County, North Carolina

............6 Olive Boston

..........5 Benjamin F Boston b: 1901 in Martin County, North Carolina

+ Hattie Wallace b: 1902 in Martin County, North Carolina, m: 1920 in Martin County, North Carolina

..........5 David Boston b: 1903 in Martín Colman, Buenos Aires, Argentina

..........5 James E Boston b: 1904 in Martin County, North Carolina, d: 1961 in Martin County, North Carolina

+ Merrcy D Moore b: 1906 in Martin County, North Carolina, m: 1925

..........5 Irene Boston b: 1906 in Martin County, North Carolina

+ Nathaniel Bonds b: 1903 in Martin County, North Carolina

..........5 Sara E Boston b: 1906, d: 1938 in Martin County, North Carolina

..........5 Noah F Boston b: 1910 in Martin County, North Carolina, d: 1972 in Philadelphia, Pennsyvania

+ Virginia b: 1910 in North Carolina

..........5 Sylvania Boston b: 1910 in Martin County, North Carolina, d: 1930

+ Homer H Gee b: 1903 in Martin County, North Carolina; ., m: 1924

..........5 Ophelia Boston b: 1913 in Martin County, North Carolina, d: 1980 in Brooklyn, Kings, New York, USA

+ Elmond A James b: 1912 in Martin County, North Carolina, m: 1933

...2 Milley Keys b: 1790 in Blounts Creek, Beaufort, North Carolina, USA

+ [unknown spouse]

......3 Milly Keys b: 1805 in Beaufort County North Carolina

Reference

Ancestry.com, United States Federal Census, 1790-1940

North Carolina Archives, Raleigh, N.C.

Heinegg, Paul. *Free African American of North Carolina, Virginia and South Carolina from the Colonial Period to about 1820.*

Article XIV of the North Carolina Constitution

Revised Statues of the State of North Carolina Chapters 1 and 5

Richard Hayes Phillips, *White Slaves Children of Colonial Maryland and Virginia: Birth and Shipping Records.*

Wikipedia, *The Free Encyclopedia*

Bunyon Keys, *Over Three Hundred Years of Black People in Blounts Creek, Beaufort County, North Carolina, Book I*

Beaufort County Marriage Records 1851-1866

Death Certificates

Surname Data Base from the Internet Last Name Origin

Old World Tree

Interviews of Many Senior Citizens Of Beaufort County

Three Special Cousins in alphabetical order by first names:

(1) Ed Lewis

(2) Selma Alston

(3) Shelia Canteen

Earl Lee Keyes Oden, a special Aunt, who at this publication is 95 years old

Printed in the United States
By Bookmasters